The
FAMILY MANAGER'S
GUIDE *to*
SUMMER
SURVIVAL

The
FAMILY MANAGER'S
GUIDE *to*
SUMMER
SURVIVAL

Kathy Peel

FAIR WINDS
PRESS
GLOUCESTER, MASSACHUSETTS

First published in the USA in 2006 by
Fair Winds Press, a member of
Quayside Publishing Group
33 Commercial Street
Gloucester, MA 01930

10 09 08 07 06   3 4 5

ISBN 1-59233-200-5

Library of Congress Cataloging-in-Publication Data

Peel, Kathy, 1951-
  The family manager's guide to summer survival / Kathy Peel.
      p. cm.
   ISBN 1-59233-200-5
  1. Family recreation. 2. Amusements. 3. Games. I. Title.
   GV182.8P35 2006
   790.1'91—dc22

                                                    2005033990

Illustrations by Lauren Scheuer
Book design by *tabula rasa* graphic design

Printed and bound in USA

Contents

A Message from Kathy

"Summer's lease hath all too short a date."

—William Shakespeare

IN 1988, I STEPPED OUT ON A LONG-HELD DREAM to write a book. Over the years I'd collected hundreds of ideas for keeping my own kids creatively occupied and helping them develop in positive ways during their summer break, and I wanted to share what I'd learned. In a moment of weakness, my husband, Bill, agreed to help me self-publish a book that would help moms survive and kids thrive during the long, hot days of summer.

Excitedly I called a friend, Joy Mahaffey, who had taught a summertime workshop for moms at her church, and invited her to join us in what seemed to many people a crazy endeavor. The first copies of *A Mother's Manual for Summer Survival* rolled off the press March 31, 1988, and nine weeks later we had sold 15,000 copies out of our living room. Six months later I signed a contract with Focus on the Family Publishing to rerelease the book in the spring of 1989. It became an instant best seller, selling over 375,000 copies before going out of print in 1996. Every year since, I've been bombarded with requests from moms in search of hard-to-find copies of the book.

Now, I am thrilled to offer you the new expanded and updated *The Family Manager's Guide to Summer Survival*. It's filled with fun ideas and suggestions—guaranteed to put a smile on any kid's face. Just keep the book handy and use these tried-and-true strategies to keep your family happily occupied, and help you turn summertime into a rewarding adventure instead of a harrowing ordeal.

May this summer be a record breaker—one in which you hear a record low of those seven dreaded words: "Mom, I'm bored. What can I do?"

Warm wishes for a kid-happy summer.

The Family Manager's Creed

I oversee the most important organization in the world—

Where hundreds of decisions are made daily

Where property and resources are managed

Where health and nutritional needs are determined

Where finances and futures are discussed and debated

Where projects are planned and events are arranged

Where transportation and scheduling are critical

Where team-building is a priority

Where careers begin and end

I am a Family Manager.

CHAPTER ONE

Planning for Success

"To affect the quality of the day, that is the highest of arts."

—Henry David Thoreau

IT'S TRUE. "BACK TO HOME" IN JUNE is just as big a deal as "back to school" in the fall.

Kids don't turn off their eyes, ears, and minds when school's out, but they continue to learn and develop in June, July, and August as well. These months are ripe with opportunity for you to help your kids grow in positive ways, to explore and learn new things together, and to make positive memories that will last a lifetime.

But a great summer won't just happen. Think of it like this: Before you begin a trip, you determine your destination and create a plan to get there. You need to do the same for your children's vacation. The ideas and strategies in this section will help you plan a super summer for your kids. *You can* turn tedium into joy without acquiring an advanced degree in childhood development or buying extraordinary supplies—and without ending up in the moms' ward of the Home for the Frantically Flustered before Labor Day! Here's how:

AIM HIGH. Think about how you would like to see your kids develop this summer, and keep this in mind: If you aim for nothing, it's likely that you'll hit it.

What qualities could you enhance this summer? When my boys were young, I used a verse from the Bible to help me come up with four developmental areas in which I could enhance their growth. Luke 2:52 says that when Jesus was a young boy, he grew in *wisdom* (intellectually), *stature* (physically), *favor with God* (spiritually), and *favor with man* (socially). Think about where your children are in each of these areas; then use the **Summertime Development Chart** on page 18 to help you set some goals and nudge your kids toward them so they'll go back to school smarter, happier, and more confident than they were when they came home in June.

CONSULT THE EXPERTS. Convene a family council before summer begins, and talk about ideas for goals for each child. Using the **Ideas for Summer Fun and Learning** list on page 19, ask your kids what they would most like to be doing and learning about. What special abilities or interests would they like to develop? Even preschoolers will have ideas.

SET ASIDE TIME TO PLAN. After your kids have voiced their desires and opinions, find some quiet time when you (both parents, if married) can make a list of potential summer activities that are in harmony with your goals for your children's growth, their desires and interests, your budget and resources, and your own time and availability. Use your list along with the ideas on pages 15–17 to help you plan fun activities for each week and each day. The **Weekly Planner** and **Summer Daily Hit List** pages 22–23 will help you organize your ideas and activities and plan each day with your children's developmental goals in mind. Include free time every day so your kids (and you) don't feel schedule bound, and make sure you schedule time for yourself. Also plan some activities with other moms and kids so you have adult company while you do "kid stuff."

 "A schedule defends from chaos and whim. It is a net for catching days . . . ." —Annie Dillard

BE FLEXIBLE. Don't be rigid about the summer schedule or expect perfection. Be ready with Plan B because what looks doable at the beginning of the week may not be right when Friday arrives. At the same time, making promises that can't be kept is a real disappointment to children. When an activity has to be changed suddenly, talk about why the plans had to change.

NETWORK AND MAXIMIZE YOUR RESOURCES. Wise family management begins with realizing that you cannot do everything yourself. Network with other parents and maximize resources in your community. As you consider what this means in terms of planning a great summer for your kids, consider these ideas:

- Group activities with other parents from your neighborhood or church. For example, sponsor a group picnic and have family games for all ages.

- Share responsibility for home classes. Trade out lessons with parents with different abilities and gifts from yours. If you enjoy baking, schedule a time to show your child and theirs how to bake a great cake. If you've got a green thumb, host a session with the kids about gardening or plant care. Another parent could hold a sewing or woodworking class or teach pre-teen girls about skin care and makeup.

- Teach swapping and bartering. Find a few parents who want to participate in a toy-swapping club. Trade toys your kids don't mind living without for a couple of weeks. The kids will love having different toys often, you'll save money not buying new ones, and the kids will learn the power of bartering. You can also host a neighborhood swap party for videos, costume jewelry, tools, children's or women's clothing, or kitchen utensils. Everyone gets the items she needs without money changing hands.

- Investigate children's programs in your area, including:
  - Summer classes offered through your local library, museum, YMCA, Jewish community center, boys or girls clubs, community colleges, or parks and recreation departments.
  - Vacation Bible school and youth programs offered by churches and synagogues.
  - Sports programs offered by schools, gyms, or clubs.
  - Summer camps. Everybody needs a break—including your kids. There are many excellent camps across America, including those run by churches, religious organizations, and athletic associations.

"Always bear in mind that your own resolution to success is more important than any other one thing." —Abraham Lincoln

A DOZEN TIPS FOR MAKING YOUR PLAN WORK

1. Be sensitive to the fact that kids need time to decompress after the stress and structure of nine months of school. Give them time for extra rest and adjustment the first couple of days after school's out.

2. Have a summer-launching dinner or event—a special time that indicates to your children that a new, fun, and interesting season of life is beginning.

3. Make necessary adjustments to your house rules. Talk about bedtimes or cur-fews; afternoon naps or quiet times; chores; how much time will be allowed for television, computer, and video games, and so on.

4. See which activities need advance planning, and make the necessary arrange-ments in plenty of time.

5. Each week, make a list of any supplies you will need. Collect or purchase them beforehand.

6. Designate and organize places for items and equipment you'll use often. For example, have a shelf or plastic bin for paint and craft clothes for kids to wear while doing messy projects; keep swimming and water-play items—beach towels, sunscreen, floating toys, flip-flops, goggles—in one convenient place; store yard-game equipment—Frisbees, horseshoes, badminton and croquet gear—in one area in the garage; keep hamburger/hot dog condiments—ketchup, mustard, mayonnaise, relish—in a plastic tote in your refrigerator for fast retrieval; put paper plates, cups, napkins, plastic utensils, unbreakable salt and pepper shakers, and a tray near the back door for quick table-setting out-side; stock your picnic basket with disposable dishes and utensils for im-promptu picnics and park outings.

7. Purchase a large thermos and plenty of small paper cups. Fill the thermos with ice water every morning and put it on your porch or in your garage so kids don't have to come in the house every time they want a drink of water. (Put a trash can nearby, too.) Keep an extra bag of ice on hand in the freezer—ready for extra-warm days or a sudden urge for homemade ice cream.

 Establish a certain time for kids to check in for dinner so you don't have to negotiate a new time every day.

8. Check in with your kids weekly. Is any activity boring, too hard, or too com-plicated? Expect that some ideas just won't work—which is why you want to stay armed and ready with plenty more.

9. If you have another full- or part-time job besides your job as Family Manager, summer can be especially challenging. Discuss your summer goals with your sitter or nanny, then work together to plan activities and excursions. Make sure you get a daily report from both the sitter and your kids in order to en-

sure that they aren't "tubing out" in front of the TV or computer and are getting plenty of opportunities to exercise their imaginations and their bodies.

10. If your children will be in day care, choose one that comes closest to meeting your objectives. Discuss with the center what goals you have for your children and see what you can do to help accomplish them.

11. If your kids are old enough to stay alone, communicate clearly what you expect of them while you are gone. It's crucial that you listen to their goals as well and help them plan to meet them. Assist them in setting goals for each day that contribute to their growth.

12. If at all possible, arrange to take some vacation days for "at home" time. Use those days to do special projects or go on field trips with your children.

For Safety's Sake
Invite parents in your neighborhood over for coffee and discuss how you can work together to make your neighborhood a safer place for outdoor play. Create a master contact list so you can call or e-mail each other to report anything suspicious. Designate "safe" houses where children may go if they are being harassed.

Summertime Development Chart

Intellectual	Physical	Spiritual	Social
Name: Elizabeth			
Goals: Improve reading skills	Improve swimming skills	Learn about God's perspective on friendship	Learn proper table manners
Ideas: • Create reading rewards program • Schedule daily reading time	Complete two weeks of advanced swimming and diving lessons	• Study verses about friendship in the Bible • Do something each	• Talk to other moms about creating a fun class about manners • Host end-of-summer tea to practice
Name:			
Goals:			
Ideas:			
Name:			
Goals:			
Ideas:			
Name:			
Goals:			
Ideas:			

Ideas for Summer Fun and Learning

Ask your kids to rate the following activities so you can consider their preferences.

Physical Activities	Awsome!	Okay	Boring
Archery	_____	_____	_____
Baseball, softball	_____	_____	_____
Badminton	_____	_____	_____
Baton twirling	_____	_____	_____
Bicycling	_____	_____	_____
Boating	_____	_____	_____
Bowling	_____	_____	_____
Cheerleading	_____	_____	_____
Croquet	_____	_____	_____
Dancing	_____	_____	_____
Diving	_____	_____	_____
Fishing	_____	_____	_____
Gymnastics	_____	_____	_____
Hiking	_____	_____	_____
Horseback riding	_____	_____	_____
Ice skating	_____	_____	_____
Jumping rope	_____	_____	_____
Kayaking	_____	_____	_____
Kite flying	_____	_____	_____
Lacrosse	_____	_____	_____
Roller-blading	_____	_____	_____
Rowing	_____	_____	_____
Running and track	_____	_____	_____
Sailing	_____	_____	_____
Soccer	_____	_____	_____
Swimming	_____	_____	_____
Tennis	_____	_____	_____
Water games	_____	_____	_____
Water skiing, water sliding	_____	_____	_____

Fun Learning Activities			
Animals—adopt and care for one	_____	_____	_____
Building models	_____	_____	_____
Building birdhouses or other simple carpentry projects	_____	_____	_____
Chess—learn to play this or other mind-stretching games	_____	_____	_____
Collecting—baseball cards, coins, dolls, shells, or stamps	_____	_____	_____
Computer games and programs	_____	_____	_____

Fun Learning Activities (continued)	Awsome!	Okay	Boring
Doll and dollhouse making	_____	_____	_____
Drama or stage production	_____	_____	_____
Drawing and illustrating stories	_____	_____	_____
Film—make home videos	_____	_____	_____
Foreign language—learn one	_____	_____	_____
Humor—write jokes, tell riddles, read and draw comics	_____	_____	_____
Inventions—make new things	_____	_____	_____
Library story hours	_____	_____	_____
Mask making	_____	_____	_____
Musical Instrument lessons	_____	_____	_____
Performing magic tricks	_____	_____	_____
Photography	_____	_____	_____
Planting a garden—vegetable, flower, or herb	_____	_____	_____
Puppet making	_____	_____	_____
Puzzle making	_____	_____	_____
Research your town and its activities	_____	_____	_____
Sewing	_____	_____	_____
Sign language	_____	_____	_____
Watercolor painting	_____	_____	_____
Writing	_____	_____	_____

Outdoor and Nature Activities

	Awsome!	Okay	Boring
Animal farm or shelter— study the animals	_____	_____	_____
Astronomy—learn about the stars	_____	_____	_____
Beach-walking, building sand castles, and studying marine life	_____	_____	_____
Bird feeder—build one and record the types of birds who use it	_____	_____	_____
Forest and wood life—explore it	_____	_____	_____
Geology—collect, identify, and polish rocks	_____	_____	_____
Nature centers—attend a local program and crafts class	_____	_____	_____
Science—attend classes and workshops at museums and planetarium	_____	_____	_____
Zoo—visit and study the animals	_____	_____	_____

Fun Places to Go

	Awsome!	Okay	Boring
Airport	_____	_____	_____
Aquarium	_____	_____	_____

Fun Places to Go (continued)	**Awsome!**	**Okay**	**Boring**
Bakery	_____	_____	_____
Beach	_____	_____	_____
Bottling company	_____	_____	_____
Campsite	_____	_____	_____
Candy factory	_____	_____	_____
Church that has a different kind of worship service than your own	_____	_____	_____
Circus	_____	_____	_____
Concert	_____	_____	_____
County fair	_____	_____	_____
Courthouse or state capitol	_____	_____	_____
Dance recital	_____	_____	_____
Farmer's market	_____	_____	_____
Fireworks display	_____	_____	_____
Fish hatchery	_____	_____	_____
Garage sale or flea market	_____	_____	_____
Greenhouse or botanical garden	_____	_____	_____
Historical site	_____	_____	_____
Ice-cream factory	_____	_____	_____
Lake or duck pond	_____	_____	_____
Library	_____	_____	_____
Local newspaper plant—ask if they give public tours	_____	_____	_____
Magic or juggling show	_____	_____	_____
Museum	_____	_____	_____
Dairy farm	_____	_____	_____
Nature reserve	_____	_____	_____
Parades	_____	_____	_____
Parents' place of work	_____	_____	_____
Parks—amusement, theme, water, or nature	_____	_____	_____
Planetarium	_____	_____	_____
Political rally	_____	_____	_____
Puppet show	_____	_____	_____
Radio or television station—call ahead and ask if you can watch a broadcast	_____	_____	_____
River or seaport	_____	_____	_____
Sports event	_____	_____	_____
Theater	_____	_____	_____
Top of the highest building near you— see what landmarks you can spot	_____	_____	_____
Zoo	_____	_____	_____

Weekly Planner

	Daily Activities	Supplies Needed
Sunday		
Monday		
Tuesday		
Wednesday		
Thursday		
Friday		
Saturday		
Special Activities		
Family/Friends to See		
Rainy Day Options		
Reading Goals		

Summer Daily Hit List™

SCHEDULE:

7:00 ....

8:00 ....

9:00 ....

10:00 ....

11:00 ....

Noon ....

1:00 ....

2:00 ....

3:00 ....

4:00 ....

5:00 ....

6:00 ....

7:00 ....

8:00 ....

PHYSICAL	INTELLECTUAL	SPIRITUAL
SOCIAL	**OUTINGS**	**ACTIVITES**

NOTES

Supplies

SUMMER HOUSE RULES

Having a set of summertime house rules was a big help to our family when our boys were young. Everyone knew what to expect, and what was expected of him. Creating your own set of house rules this summer will help you create a more peaceful environment in your home, maintain some semblance of order, and save a lot of emotional wear and tear. In addition to keeping their belongings picked up, cleaning up after themselves in the kitchen, hanging up their wet swimsuits and towels to dry, and such, here are ideas for other rules you may want to adopt for a more peaceful summer.

1. No yelling at anyone or "pitching fits." Reserve yelling and screaming for emergencies only. "Outside voices" are not to be used inside, and pitching a fit to get something is not acceptable behavior. Never give the desired response when a child pitches a fit as a means of getting it.

2. Calling names, or making unkind, cutting remarks to each other is strictly out of order. Make a list of the names and negative phrases you would like to eliminate from your children's vocabulary, such as "Shut up," "dummy," "stupid," "You make me sick."

3. Take responsibility for your own actions and words. Kids need to know that you hold them responsible for their actions—no matter what the other person does.

   Consider setting a certain time of day for tattling and complaining. If children know they have to wait until, say, five o'clock to grumble or snitch on a sibling (unless the situation is dangerous) it's amazing how many issues get resolved on their own.

4. Respect each other's space and stuff. Create guidelines for walking into each other's bedrooms and borrowing each other's belongings. Outline consequences ahead of time when children mistreat the property of others.

5. Abide by family chore system. Everyone who lives under the roof of a house should help with the upkeep—and when kids are out of school they can do more to help out. Create a chore chart so you'll know who's supposed to do what when.

CHAPTER TWO

Fun Summer Learning: The Three Rs and Beyond

"Most learning is not the result of instruction. It is rather the result of unhampered participation in a meaningful setting."

—Ivan Illich

IF YOU SUDDENLY WON THE LOTTERY or inherited a large sum of money and were able to hire a full-time cook, housekeeper, chauffeur, gardener, handyman, accountant, and secretary, you'd have lots of your family bases covered. But there's one department you'd still have to oversee personally: your children's education.

In my mind, teachers deserve a special place in heaven. They work long hours, need an extra measure of patience to do their job, and they need our support as parents to help them do it well. Summer is a great time to do just this.

There are tons of fun ways you can reinforce academic basics—reading, writing, and arithmetic—so your kids won't lose the academic skills they learned in the classroom and will have a leg up when they start school again in the fall. Here are some ideas to get your creative juices flowing.

1. Establish "Kids in the Kitchen" night. Let your children use simple cookbooks to create a menu for dinner. With appropriate supervision, they could try a different combination of recipes every week. They'll use reading and math to follow recipes. They can exercise creativity by making menus and place mats with the name or logo of their "restaurant."

2. Have a toy sale. Ask neighborhood children to look for toys they never use or have outgrown. Children can design posters to advertise the sale, decide on prices, and run the sale. They can then deliver the profits (or a

portion thereof) to a shelter for homeless families. They'll learn a lot about relationships and working together, and they'll use their math and planning skills to get everything organized.

3. Help your kids organize a neighborhood Fourth of July parade. Research historical characters and costumes in an encyclopedia, on the Internet, or at your local library. Invite the neighbors to join in. Give small prizes for the most historically accurate costumes, for the funniest, and so on. Make sure everybody's efforts get recognized. Or, as an alternative to a Fourth of July parade, have a pageant. Kids can act out scenes from history— Boston Tea Party, Washington crossing the Delaware, the signing of the Declaration of Independence. They can research, write the script (which they could read or memorize), and make costumes.

4. Reinforce writing skills by encouraging kids to write to their grandparents, aunts and uncles, cousins, even friends. In doing so they are practicing writing and reading; plus they're learning about their responsibility in keeping up relationships with family at a distance. Even the most reluctant readers and writers might enjoy e-mail correspondence.

5. Have your child make her own code with numbers representing letters. Send coded messages to friends.

6. Give your child a list of twenty items to find in the newspaper. See how long it takes to find the items on the list.

7. Play the stock market. Give each of your children $500 worth of play money and help them "buy" stocks listed on the financial page of the newspaper. Keep track of all purchases and sales. Check the financial page each day, comparing the ups and downs of their stocks. Let them buy and sell to try to recoup lost money or make more. Not least among the new skills they'll learn are the benefits and pitfalls of risk taking.

"Satisfaction of one's curiosity is one of the greatest sources of happiness in life." —Linus Pauling

8. Take a challenging trip to the zoo. Before you go, use an encyclopedia to look up animals you will see, and make a list of their scientific names. Have your child try to locate each animal by using this list of names and matching them to the scientific names on the cages.

9. Buy a tree-identification book or check one out of the library. Go on an outing and, together, identify the trees in your region.

10. Take a ride on a bus, train, or subway. Have your child record the experience by writing a travel journal about where you go and what you see and do. This is an opportunity for your child to polish their observational and writing skills.

11. Take a drive to locate and read historical markers in your area. See what happened in years past right where you live.

12. Visit the state house. Watch legislators debate, view the governor's office, and listen to the clerk explain how a bill becomes law. Call beforehand to make sure congress is in session. Some states allow older children to be pages on the chamber floor. Ask how to sign up your kids if they're interested.

13. Learn while you travel. Teach your kids how to read a map or atlas. As they begin to understand road systems, show them where you live and where you will have your vacation this year. Ask them to add up the miles between different points. Have them figure out what would be a shorter route between Point A and Point B. Ask them: How much farther would it be if we stopped at a certain point of interest? If we average 60 mph, how long will it take to get there? How many rivers will we cross? What is the highest mountain we will cross?

14. Sponsor a neighborhood invention convention. Encourage your kids to invent a new product or a variation of an old one. They can sell or take orders for their inventions the day they're displayed. For example, an elementary-school-age girl's hair kept getting caught in the back of the chair when she worked at her desk. She made a fabric cover with ties for the chair back. Our boys invented a batting tee from PVC pipe.

"Imagination is more important than knowledge."
—Albert Einstein

15. Promote summer reading. Experts say kids need to read about twenty minutes a day if they want to maintain their reading skills. Good books not only entertain children but also expand their worlds. Reading exposes them to different cultures, interesting ideas, language skills, and new vocabulary words. Their imagination and creativity grow along with their reading skills and ability to solve problems. Sometimes kids need

Win-Win Solution for Saving Artwork
Wondering what to do with the piles of artwork your child doesn't want to part with at the end of the year? Work together to scan them into your computer and use them as your screensavers. Your child's masterpieces are "stored" in a safe place, and he will love seeing some of them on your screen. Best of all, you'll have less paper clutter to deal with.

incentives to help them discover the joy of reading. Here are a few ways to encourage your children to build good reading habits this summer.

- Start a summer reading club with some of your children's friends. Charge a small fee to join and use the money to buy a gift certificate at your favorite bookstore for the one who reads the most books. At the end of the summer, announce the winner and award the prize. Present reading certificates to all who participated.

- Encourage children to write a letter to a favorite author. Send the letter to the author's publisher, requesting that the letter be forwarded to the author. (Check copyright page of author's book for publisher's address.) Many authors will write back.

- Get everyone in your family a library card and visit the library regularly.

- Set a good example in your own reading habits. Let them see you reading good books and articles often.

- Enjoy good books together as a family. Read aloud to children of all ages. Reading with enthusiasm and excitement will heighten their curiosity and maintain their interest.

- Create a reward chart for a summer reading program. Have younger children start reading ten to fifteen minutes a day, gradually increasing the time. You can start older children off at thirty minutes a day. When my boys were growing up, I made colorful charts that set weekly reading goals for them. A reward at the end of each week was a great incentive.

- Play reading charades. Write the titles of books on slips of paper, choosing ones your children know. Fold the papers, and put them in a basket. One person draws a slip of paper and pantomimes the title. Whoever guesses the correct title has the next turn.

TECH TOGETHERNESS

Computers are becoming an important way children—at increasingly younger ages—learn and interact with their friends as well as the world at large. If you feel like your kids are passing you by when it comes to technology and the Internet, use the summer months to let your child bring you up to speed, teaching you what he's learning to do in school on a computer. It's a great way to not only sharpen your skills, but build your child's self-esteem—"I'm teaching my mom to use a computer!"—and spend focused time together. Quality multitasking at its best!

Becoming a computer-savvy mom is also important for your child's safety. You need to install filtering devices on your computer so you can supervise the Web sites your child visits and control unwanted e-mail. Be careful about games that can be downloaded off the Internet, as many of them are violent and contain sexual content. Oversee and limit the time your child spends chatting with friends and instant messaging. Instruct your child to never give out personal information such as his full name, address, phone numbers, activities, passwords, and such. Make it crystal clear that conversations with strangers can be extremely dangerous.

Here are a few ideas to get your creative juices flowing about computer projects to tackle together:

- Research your family roots, types of pets you're considering, summer camps, vacation spots, biographies of people you admire.
- Compare prices on something your child wants to buy for herself or as a Father's Day gift for Dad.
- Find directions for embarking on a new hobby such as origami, coin collecting, or cross-stitch.
- Learn to save photos and set up files for viewing.
- Create a newsletter about what's going on in your family and send it to extended-family members.
- Learn about the geography and historical significance of a place to which you're traveling.
- Read about the culture of a country on the other side of the world.
- Search for printable coupons from local businesses and restaurants.
- Read about emergency preparedness for your home, then gather supplies.
- Find kid-friendly recipes and start a file of favorites.
- Create personalized stationary or a logo for your family.
- Learn to send free e-invitations and greeting cards.

FINDING A GOOD SUMMER CAMP

I'm a big believer in sending kids to summer camp. Going away to camp teaches children flexibility, independence, and responsibility, and can help them develop social skills as well as grow mentally, physically, and spiritually. At camp, children can observe positive role models and broaden their understanding of people from different walks of life.

Finding a camp that's a good fit for your child can take time, so start early. When researching camp options, there are important questions you should ask. How the camp staff answers these questions will help you make a good decision and help protect your child—and you—from a miserable camping experience.

- 💡 What is the camp's philosophy? Is it centered on sports, religion, art, music, outdoor adventure? Make sure the camp's focus is something your child loves.

- 💡 How do you choose counselors? Is each applicant screened and trained? What does this process entail?

- 💡 If a child has problems, whom can he talk to besides his counselor? Can he call home?

- 💡 Is the camp accredited by the American Camping Association? If not, why? The ACA sets standards for everything from camp management to safety.

- 💡 Is the camp prepared to provide first aid? What happens in case of a medical emergency? Will the parents be contacted? What about insurance?

- 💡 Does the camp include programs that help kids get acquainted? Since camp is made up of many strangers, this is essential to a child's comfort.

- 💡 What kind of instruction is offered at activities? How long do activities last? Make sure the activities match your child's age and attention span.

- 💡 If kids take trips as part of camp, how will they be transported?

- 💡 Which parents can we ask to tell us more about the camp? Ask the kids, too.

Packing for Camp

Don't buy brand-new clothes for your child to take to camp. It's highly likely that camp clothes will come home badly soiled, mildewed, torn, lost—or all of the above. Plus, having well-worn clothes and familiar possessions will help ease the transition, especially for first-time campers.

Most camps have a what-to-bring list, but the American Camping Association suggests the following advice for packing:

- Pack only the camper's absolute needs.
- Send durable, comfortable clothes.
- Shorts, T-shirts, and jeans are staple items.
- Write the camper's name on every item with a permanent marker or on labels.
- Pack long pants for hikes and horseback rides.
- Shoes should be comfortable and broken in.
- A raincoat or poncho is a must.
- A hat or visor is good to have.
- Pack toiletries and personal hygiene items.
- Other useful items to include are sunscreen; lip balm; insect repellent; a flashlight with extra batteries; a camera with film; a canteen or water bottle; and stamped, addressed envelopes. A stuffed animal or family photo may be a comforting reminder of home.
- Do not pack electronic toys or equipment, food, or hunting knives.
- If your child takes medication, send it in the original bottle, with dosage instructions.
- Check with the camp for specifics on sleeping bags, bedding, towels, and specialized gear. Also check on its policy about bringing spending money.

CHAPTER THREE

Dollars and Sense

"Beware of little expenses. A small leak will sink a great ship." —Benjamin Franklin

OVER THE SUMMER, WHEN MOST KIDS are making (or asking for) money, opportunities to teach them a healthy respect for money abound. Look for everyday ways to show how actions lead to consequences, and financial ones can be the most rewarding-or the most uncomfortable—of all.

- Let kids be responsible for late charges on videos. Have them start the habit of rewinding rented tapes or returning DVDs to their case immediately after watching and placing them in a designated easy-to-see location near the door. If they forget and you're charged, they can pay.

- Get everyone a library card. Before buying new books, check to see if they're available at the library. When you get home, write the due date on a central family calendar. Put a child in charge of reminding everyone of the day to gather books. If someone forgets, let him or her pay the late fee.

- Nurture low-cost hobbies and activities such as gardening, card games, walking and hiking, creating inexpensive crafts, and taking picnics. Get up early, watch the sun rise, and cook breakfast over a campfire or grill at a park. Go on a bike-hike as a family; ride to a favorite eating spot, then ride back. Call your local parks and recreation department and ask about inexpensive programs and activities that your family might enjoy. Kids can see that fun isn't necessarily expensive.

- Check out local consignment shops before buying furniture or seldom-worn clothing such as ski clothes, formal wear, and boys' blazers. Have kids compare prices so they can see your savings.

- Have your kids fix sack lunches for themselves when they're going to the pool or park. Show kids the cost of a typical lunch out—even a fast-food one—and how over weeks and months, that expenditure really drains the bank account.

- If possible, go to matinees rather than prime-time, full-price movies. Make sure kids eat before they go. Teach them how expensive concession snacks are by comparing store prices to the ones in the theater.

- Take your own rafts and life jackets to water parks or the beach. Renting these items can be expensive, so teach kids by showing them how much money you save by supplying your own equipment.

 Keep a supply of self-adhesive patches (at home and in the car) so you can repair punctured inflatable toys on the spot.

- Drink water when you eat out at restaurants. Money saved this way can add up fast if you have a big family. Let kids compute the savings while they're waiting for their meals.

- Take your family's used clothing, books, toys, and so on, to a consignment shop. Some will give you more dollars' worth in trade than in cash. Let the kids learn that exchanging is better than throwing away. (One ten-year-old boy I know started his own business selling used books and items on eBay.)

- If you can't afford to buy tickets to a special concert or play, find out if you can attend a rehearsal. Show kids that money isn't the only ticket to fun.

- Look into joining your local YMCA or community center instead of a fancy health club; they often provide the same services for a lot less. Compare prices and features, and let your kids see the results.

- Have kids clip and organize coupons, and let them keep any money saved. Make sure they check and highlight expiration dates—a good activity to do while watching TV.

- When shopping for groceries, ask older kids to bring along a calculator and add up the price of everything you put into your shopping cart.

- Help kids learn the consequences of being irresponsible. Let them know that if they leave their bikes in the rain, toys in the yard, or glasses at the pool and these items are broken, destroyed, or stolen, you will not automatically replace them. If your child breaks (even accidentally) another child's toy, make your child, as the responsible party, help pay for a replacement.

Value-Added Outing

Summer is a good time to go to the bank with your teenager and open a checking account for her. Set up a budget and help her manage her own money.

CHAPTER FOUR

Beyond Babysitting: Super Summer Jobs

"Opportunity is missed by most people because it is dressed in overalls and looks like work."

—Thomas Edison

STARTING FROM THE TIME OUR TWO OLDEST boys were nine and five, they had to earn and save money for big purchases and summer camp. In those early days they had flower-bulb-selling and porch- and driveway-sweeping businesses. As they grew they worked at odd jobs and ran their own businesses, and they also acquired great experience: They learned to communicate with adults in a professional manner, realized the importance of being responsible when working for others, and discovered creative ways to advertise. They also learned to delay gratification, found out how to make good financial decisions, and acquired an appreciation for what things cost. Finally, they experienced the satisfaction of knowing what it is to do a job well. Now that they're adults, the lessons they learned are still paying off as business owners.

Begin a business by brainstorming about the types of services or products your kids can offer. Check with local government offices to see if a business license or permit is needed. Then create an advertising flyer or a business card to distribute to homes or post on public bulletin boards. Let the following inspire your own ideas:

- Aid the elderly—do their shopping, run errands.
- Bake and sell homemade bread and cookies.
- Be a birthday clown.
- Caddie for a golfer.

- Clean carpets.
- Clean houses or move furniture.
- Clean swimming pools.
- Clear away old junk and trash.
- Distribute flyers for local small businesses.
- Bathe and groom pets.
- Help people move—pack and clean up.
- Hold a garage sale.
- Iron clothes.
- Make and paint signs.
- Mow lawns.
- Offer a messenger service.
- Paint outdoor furniture, fences, doghouses, porches, decks, storage sheds.
- Paint house numbers on curbs with stencils.
- Pet-sit. Many working adults are delighted to pay someone else to give their pet care and affection or to walk their dog while they're at work.
- Plan and host birthday parties. Older kids can help parents give birthday parties for small children. They can dress up like a party-theme character, help with crafts, organize and oversee games, pass out food, pick up trash, and help watch for small guests who might wander off.
- Plant a pumpkin patch. Sell the pumpkins in October.
- Produce a backyard carnival and sell tickets for the games and refreshments.
- Publish a neighborhood newspaper or newsletter. Collect information about opportunities in your community—who has what for sale, services or items that neighbors would like to trade—and other facts of interest to the people in your area. Type up the information and make copies to sell to neighbors.
- Pull weeds.
- Put on a backyard day camp.
- Rake leaves.
- Repair bikes.
- Run an errand service, including grocery and dry-cleaning delivery.
- Start an odd-job service. Advertise by passing out flyers in the neighborhood.

- Sweep porches and driveways.
- Tend and entertain younger children.
- Tutor younger children in reading.
- Type, do word processing.
- Wash cars. Try an on-the-spot car wash. Kids can go door-to-door carrying cloths, buckets, window spray, whisk broom, and portable minivacuum.
- Wash windows.
- Water plants and yards for vacationing families.

"When men are employed, they are best contented; for on the days they worked they were good-natured and cheerful, and, with the consciousness of having done a good day's work, they spent the evening jollily; but on our idle days they were mutinous and quarrelsome." —Benjamin Franklin

HOW TO MAKE FRIENDS AND INFLUENCE CLIENTS

Be sensitive about what kinds of jobs your kids will feel comfortable performing. An outgoing child won't mind going door-to-door, drumming up business from neighbors. But a shy child may feel threatened at the thought of talking to an adult one-on-one. Teaching your children some simple communication skills can bolster their courage and help them make a good impression on potential customers.

1. Have a neat appearance. An adult is more likely to want to hire a well-groomed child with clean clothes and combed hair.

2. Make good eye contact, and shake hands firmly. Have your child practice looking directly into your eyes while talking. People are more likely to trust someone who will look them in the eye. Practice a firm handshake. This sends the signal that your child has a good self-image and takes his or her business seriously.

3. Give a clear, concise message describing services or products. Help your child write down exact words. Pretend you are the customer and role-play

the situation until your child has memorized the lines and feels comfortable saying them.

4. Smile and be courteous—even if you get turned down. A person who says no today may call later.

5. Exceed expectations.

 "Nine out of ten of the rich men of our country today, started out in life as poor boys, with determined wills, industry, perseverance, economy and good habits." —P. T. Barnum

CHAPTER FIVE

Ladies and Gentlemen,

*"Good manners are the technique
of expressing consideration
for the feelings of others."*

—Alice Duer Miller

GOOD MANNERS DO MORE THAN MAKE CHILDREN pleasant to have around; they equip your kids to face varied social situations successfully. But instilling good manners has always been a challenge. Here's what Socrates said regarding the young people of Athens in 500 B.C.

Youth today loves luxury. They have bad manners, contempt for authority, no respect for older people, and talk nonsense when they should work. Young people do not stand up any longer when adults enter the room. They contradict their parents, talk too much in company, guzzle their food, lay their legs on the table, and tyrannize their elders.

Summertime is a good time to work on manners and teach children essential lessons for getting along in the world. Remember to avoid nagging—be gentle and consistent instead. And don't forget to affirm kids whenever they get it right!

- Practice good introduction manners: Teach your child to stand and shake hands with adults when meeting them for the first time.
- Teach your child to say "Excuse me?" if she doesn't hear what someone is saying.
- Make sure your children arrive on time at special occasions and activities. Instruct them to call a host if lateness is unavoidable.

- ☀ Teach your child to be sensitive to the loner at a party, to invite him or her to participate or to talk.
- ☀ Instruct your child to offer kitchen help, to keep his belongings organized, and to tidy up the bathroom when visiting another child's home.
- ☀ Be sure your child says "Thank you" after visiting someone.
- ☀ If the visit was special in some way, or lasted longer than a night, work with your child on a thank-you note to mail the hosts.

Mealtime etiquette is important. Teach kids to:

- ☀ Sit up straight.
- ☀ Be quiet—don't drag your chair across the floor or bang silverware against your plate.
- ☀ Keep a napkin in your lap, and don't forget to use it.
- ☀ Keep chair legs on the floor.
- ☀ If the family you're visiting says grace, follow their custom.
- ☀ Pass condiments around, not across, the table.
- ☀ Don't start eating until everyone has been served.
- ☀ Ask the person closest to what you want to "please pass" it. Thank him or her for doing so.
- ☀ Take small portions. Help yourself to seconds after everyone has been served.
- ☀ Take what you're offered. If you don't like something, politely say "No, thank you" or take a very small portion.
- ☀ Eat slowly. Put down your spoon or fork between bites.
- ☀ Chew with your mouth closed.
- ☀ Talk only after you've swallowed your food.
- ☀ Take small bites.
- ☀ Swallow food before taking a drink.
- ☀ If food is stuck in your teeth, remove it privately after the meal.
- ☀ Keep elbows and arms off of the table.
- ☀ Ask to be excused when the meal is over.

Swine Fine!

To help teach my boys manners one summer, I initiated the "Swine Fine" rule. Before I found the perfect piggy bank to suit my purposes, I painted a picture of a pig on the top of a white plastic bucket and put it on my kitchen counter. Whenever one of the boys behaved disrespectfully toward a family member or exhibited poor manners, I called out "Swine fine!" He was required to deposit a designated amount of change (which I got to keep) in my bucket. For total buy-in into your program, let your kids create a bank or bucket and call "Swine fine" on Mom and Dad, too!

Flag Etiquette

Summertime patriotic holidays—Memorial Day, Flag Day and July the Fourth—provide a natural opportunity to teach children flag etiquette. Even young children can be taught that our flag is special, and we treat it with respect. The National Flag Foundation lists some simple rules for honoring our flag.

- You can wear a T-shirt *showing* a flag; do not wear clothes *made of flags*.

- Do not wear pants or use towels bearing flags—the flag should not be sat upon.

- Raise a flag in a lively manner; lower it slowly.

- Don't create a flag motif on a lawn or football field, where feet can step on it.

- Don't hang a flag at night unless you can illuminate it.

- Don't display a flag during snow, rain, or other storms unless it is weatherproof.

- Hung vertically, the star-studded section should be in observers' top left corner.

CHAPTER SIX

Family Fitness

"It is remarkable how one's wits are sharpened by physical exercise."

—Pliny the Younger

SUMMERS ARE A GREAT TIME TO SET nutritional and physical-fitness goals for your family, and to begin some new routines. Meet together and decide on a healthy-eating plan and an exercise program that fits your family's schedule and ability level.

1. Create a colorful chart that teaches younger children the basic food groups and talk about what we need to eat to stay healthy. They can put a sticker on the chart when they eat a food from a particular category.

2. Ask your favorite fast-food restaurants for calorie and content information. Make up a multiple-choice quiz about the calorie count of your kids' favorite items. My kids were shocked to learn that fries, a chocolate shake, and a large cheeseburger have 1,310 calories.

"No kidding: Children will exercise if fitness equals fun." —Dr. George Sheehan

3. Schedule a family sports night once a week. Try out different sports such as basketball, bowling, racquetball, skating, or tennis.

4. Hold a family crunch contest. Record how many sit-ups each family member can do at the beginning of the summer. Do sit-ups three times a week; then at the end of summer vacation, hold another contest to see how much each person has improved.

5. Go on regular bike rides. Map your route before you leave, choosing new and interesting destinations every week.

6. Incorporate calisthenics into family cleanup time. Do lunges, fast-paced walking, and stretches while completing regular household duties.

7. Enroll in a family summer recreational program at your local YMCA or parks and recreation department.

8. Develop a family workout schedule. Here is a sample plan: Do twenty minutes of calisthenics or other strength-building exercises on Mondays. Do thirty minutes of aerobic activities like running, swimming, or walking on Wednesdays. Do fun recreational sports such as biking, hiking, or skating for one hour on Fridays.

9. Turn the playground into a gym and get fit while your tot is busy having fun. Work the equipment. Giving your child a ride on the merry-go-round will rev up your heart, firm up your arms, and strengthen your legs. Pushing her on a swing is also great for toning your arms. You can also grab a pole and do some leg lifts while she's playing in the sandbox.

10. Park at a far-off parking spot and take the opportunity to walk when you're running errands.

11. Invest in an exercise video and work out at home with your kids.

12. Take the stairs instead of the elevator.

13. Become a family of water drinkers. Daily, we lose the equivalent of ten cups of water. And you replace only about four cups through eating. Hidden dehydration robs you of energy and makes you feel lethargic. Drink water all day, every day.

14. Take vitamins. Ask your pediatrician what's right for your kids, and at the very least, you should take a multivitamin. Don't forget to talk to your doctor about what your own body needs.

"Health is not valued till sickness comes."
—Thomas Fuller

CHAPTER SEVEN

Getting a Little Help Around the House

"Mowing the lawn, Clearing the table
Kids love to help—Until they are able."

—Bill Peel

SUMMER, WINTER, SPRING, AND FALL: Kids need to help with household chores. Period. They need to see themselves as productive contributors to the welfare of the home, since they benefit from living there. Even if someone cleans your house, you should require your kids to do household chores. I encourage you to not do anything or buy anything on a regular basis for your children that they are capable of doing or buying for themselves. This will help them become independent, productive adults.

We tried to make chore time as fun as possible. Our kids never knew what to expect when we called for "cabin cleanup." Whoever had the job of folding clothes at our house got to wear the "Laundry Man" cape and mask. Sometimes we wore different hats and marched around to the great Sousa marches while cleaning. Other times we played classics or set the kitchen timer and played "Beat the Clock." (We still play Beat the Clock today when the boys come home to visit and we're all cleaning up the kitchen after a big meal. It has become a family tradition that I don't mind a bit!)

Preschoolers from two to five can do simple chores. Be sure to give them only one task at a time so you don't confuse them. Keep instructions simple and specific, such as, "Please pick up your blocks." You may need to repeat the sentence while you show your children what to do. Work alongside them until they learn how to do the task. Toddlers probably won't fold the towels as neatly as you'd like, but that's okay. It's more important that they learn to be productive.

Use **My Chore Chart** on page 50 for younger children and the **No Fail Chore Chart** on page 49 to encourage kids a little older to fulfill their responsibilities around the house. And, as you teach your children to do their fair share, keep in mind that they will not grow up remembering if the towels were perfectly folded in the linen closet or if the floors were spotless, but they *will* remember if home was a good place to be and if mom was a fun person to be with.

"Perfectionism is the voice of the oppressor, the enemy of the people. It will keep you cramped and insane your whole life." —Anne Lamott

No Fail Chore Chart

Plus Points	Minus Points
Bathe and dress baby.............................+1	Bad attitude ....-1
Clean countertops and table after dinner ....+1	Leave clothes, misc., in den........................... -1
Clean closet and hang up clothes ....+1	Leave dishes anywhere but in
Empty dishwasher ....+1	the sink when finished .... -1
Do extra chores ....+1	Leave kitchen a mess a mess
Feed dog ....+1	after making a snack ....-1
Fold one load of clothes..........................+1	Leave trash anywhere but in garbage.................-1
Load dishwasher after meal....................+1	Poor table manners...................................-1
Make bed, clean up room ....+1	
Sweep floors ....+1	
Take out garbage ....+1	
Vacuum house......................................+1	
Work in yard ....+1 or 2	

Special Rewards

Points Earned

Names				
Sunday				
Monday				
Tuesday				
Wednesday				
Thursday				
Friday				
Saturday				

My Chores

Jobs:	Sunday	Monday	Tuesday	Wednesday	Thursday	Friday	Saturday
Brush Teeth							
Dust Furniture							
Fold Laundry							
Get Newspaper							
Load Dishwasher							
Make a Bed							
Pick up Toys							
Put Away Pajamas							
Put Bikes in Garage							
Put Cups in Sink							
Set Table							
Water Plants							

CHAPTER EIGHT

Over 300 Things to Do When Kids Say, "I'm Bored!"

(OR HOW TO COMPETE WITH TELEVISION)

"Whatever you do, put romance and enthusiasm into the life of our children." —Margaret Ramsey MacDonald

CREATE A WELL-STOCKED CRAFT CABINET

It's good to be prepared when creative genius strikes by stocking up ahead of time. A large plastic bin is a great place to store craft supplies. Corral small items in resealable plastic bags. Your kids can personalize their own bin with really cool vinyl letters. Good craft items to keep on hand include:

scissors	yarn	egg cartons
tape	felt/fabric pieces	Styrofoam meat trays
glue gun	chalk	glass jars
school glue	crayons	magazines
construction paper	markers	newspapers
tissue paper	tempera, acrylic, and	popcorn (packing
stickers	fabric paint	material)
pipe cleaners	erasers	plastic soda bottles
googly eyes	sharpeners	and milk jugs
rulers/tape measure	paintbrushes	Popsicle sticks
stencils	white/colored paper	thread spools
batting for sewing	smock	toilet paper and
projects	bottle caps	paper towel tubes
fabric pens	brown paper bags	wallpaper scraps
clay	buttons and beads	pompoms
glitter	rickrack	finger paint

FRIENDLY COMPETITION

- Flying saucers: Tape two paper plates together to create a curved top and bottom. Glue a paper bowl to the center top to make a cabin for the crew. Let dry. Use markers or crayons to draw insignias, windows, doors, et cetera. Designate a landing pad, then toss flying saucers through the air. See whose lands closest to the pad.

- Recycled boats: Clean fast-food clamshell-style containers. Punch a hole through the top, near the middle. Poke a stick through the hole for the mast. Glue bottom of stick to container. Tape a sail made from construction paper to the mast. Have a race.

- Balloon catch: Blow up a balloon as big as the diameter of your kitchen funnel. Toss the balloon in the air and try to catch it in the wide mouth of the funnel.

- Flying ring toss: Trace a 12-inch (30-cm) dinner plate onto a piece of corrugated cardboard and cut it out. Then, in the center of the circle, trace another plate, about 2 inches (5 cm) smaller; cut it out, too, leaving a ring. Decorate the ring with markers or crayons. Put some water or sand into five empty 2-liter bottles (to give them weight) and mark the bottles with a point value of ten, twenty, thirty, forty, and fifty. Set up the bottles in a line, about 10 inches (25 cm) apart. Stand back a few feet and try to toss the ring so that it goes over the neck of a bottle. See how many points you can get.

- Twist up: Use chalk to draw a 10-foot (3-m) square on a paved driveway or sidewalk. Draw a lot of footprint-size ovals within the square. Players stand in the square with one foot in an oval. Each player then takes a turn telling the player on his or her right which oval to put a foot or hand in—without getting out of the original oval. Be ready for a lot of laughs.

- Tube-it: Decorate a paper-towel tube using crayons, markers, or stickers. Measure and cut a 24-inch (60-cm) piece of string. Securely tape one end of the string about 2 inches (5 cm) down inside the tube. Make a hole in the center of the bottom of an empty 8-ounce (235-ml) paper cup. Thread the other end of the string through the hole and make a knot or tape it to secure the string. Now hold the bottom of the tube and see if you call flop the cup and have it land on top of the tube. Score one point each time you do it. Player with the highest score wins.

- Target practice: Cut a 24-inch (60-cm) round hole on one side of a large box. With string, hang a foil pan from the top edge of the hole so pan swings freely in the center. Stand back; throw tennis balls at the target. Balls will collect in the box.

- Frisbee golf: Make a golf course in your backyard. Draw large numbers on paper plates and tape to trees or shrubs to designate each "hole," which players must hit with the Frisbee.

- Backyard bowling: Spray-paint ten (2 liter) soda bottles to make bowling pins. (Put a little water or sand in each to weigh it down.) Turn your driveway or patio into a bowling lane.

- Knock 'em down: Cover sixteen-ounce cans with contact paper. Stack them in pyramid formation and let kids try to knock them down with tennis balls.

- Balloon volleyball: Tie six to ten feet of string between two chairs for a net.

- Hula-hoop contest: Use a stopwatch to see who can keep the hoop spinning the longest.

- Make a toss game: Bury two tin cans flush with the ground 10 feet (3 m) apart. Get four 2-inch (5-cm) metal washers at the hardware store. Mark two washers with one color and the other two with a different color. Toss them like horseshoes. Washers that go in the can earn two points each, and the one that lands nearest the hole gets one point.

- Velcro catch: Put self-adhesive Velcro dots (available at fabric stores) around a Ping-Pong ball. Then, create a mitt by cutting an 8-inch (20 cm) circle from a piece of cardboard, and make a strap for holding it on one side. Glue an 8-inch (20-cm) felt circle on the other side. Let one person toss the ball and the other catch it with the mitt.

- Water balloon toss: For neighborhood fun, separate the kids into two parallel lines, facing each other. One line will hold the water balloons. Each kid tosses a balloon to his partner in the other line. If the partner catches it, he takes one step back and then tosses it back to his partner. If the balloon is dropped and/or breaks, that pair is out. Repeat this process until only one pair remains.

- Balloon broom hockey: Mark off opposite goals and boundary lines. Two kids or more can play the game, depending on the number of brooms you have. Bat the balloon with the broom and see who can reach his or her goal first.

- Bicycle bonanza: Set up a bicycle obstacle course. See who can ride through it the fastest.

- Beanbag toss: Make beanbags from scrap fabric. Draw a clown on an appliance box, cut a round hole for a mouth, and throw bean bags at it. The bags will collect inside the box.

- Backyard Olympics: Make medals by covering cardboard circles with foil and stapling them to different-colored ribbons.

- Pie throw: Cut a face hole in a refrigerator box for a pie throw. Load sponges with whipping cream and fire away.

- Foil ball: Start a foil ball or rubber-band ball contest at the beginning of the summer. Collect pieces of foil or rubber bands, and keep adding to the balls. Give a prize to the child who has the biggest one by the end of vacation.
- Patriot game: Make up your own Fourth of July history trivia game.
- Jacks tournament: Teach your kids this game from your childhood.

BUGGIN' OUT AND OTHER ADVENTURES IN SCIENCE

- Catch tadpoles and watch them develop. Keep them in a bucket or jar and add fresh water.
- Underwater viewer: Cut the top and bottom off a clean half-gallon milk carton. Stretch clear plastic wrap over the bottom and secure with rubber band or tape. Lower the viewer into a stream, pond, lake, or creek. Look in the open end of the milk carton and see if you can identify what's living and growing.
- Collect pinecones and soak in water for several minutes. Watch them close. Allow to dry for a few days, then watch them open.
- Observe what's living under your feet. Sit down and mark out a 1-foot (30-cm) square area of grass; have your child do the same. Name all the living things you can find. Who spotted more items?
- Preserve a spider web. Find a deserted spider web and dust it gently with talcum powder. Place a piece of black construction paper in a cardboard box; coat the paper with hair spray. While the hair spray is slightly tacky, mount the web onto the paper. Coat the paper with acrylic spray to preserve the web.
- Make homemade potpourri. In a metal colander, place flower petals, small pinecones, and bark and leaves from pine, oak, or eucalyptus trees. Place on top of water heater to dry. Add drops of perfumed oil. Remove the lid of a shallow box, decorate it with gift paper, and fill with potpourri.
- Construct a wormery. Fill a gallon-size jar with layers of various soils: garden, peat, and sand. Water thoroughly; add about eight earthworms dug from a flower bed. Scatter worms on soil surface; cover with dead leaves or grass clippings. Cover the entire jar with an opaque cloth. Sprinkle water on the surface occasionally, and check worms regularly to see how their tunnels are progressing and how the soil's layers have shifted.
- Cricket thermometer: Using a watch with a second hand, count the number of times a cricket chirps in one minute. Subtract forty from this number, and divide the answer by four. Add fifty. Check a thermometer and see how close your answer is to the outdoor temperature.

- Zoological scavenger hunt: Using facts from an encyclopedia, your children can create a list of animal riddles for each other to solve. Then take a trip to the zoo. Have them exchange lists and try to identify the animals by matching the riddle clues with the zoological information on the cages.

- Make a bug jar for catching all kinds of specimens. Punch holes in the lid of a jar, or use a rubber band to hold a piece of cloth in place for a lid. Put a crumpled, damp paper towel inside to provide moisture and crevices for the bugs to hide in and cling to. Some safe bugs to catch are walking sticks, ant lions, ladybugs, and pill bugs. Teach your child not to touch bugs that could be harmful, such as spiders, ants, wasps, and bees. Check out a bug identification book from the library to learn more.

- Bug mansion: Cut a piece of screen 1 foot (30 cm) wide and 2 inches (5 cm) longer than the circumference of two round cake pans. Make screen into a tube the same size as the pans, and tape or sew ends together. Press some modeling clay into the two pans; place one on each end of the screen. (Clay secures the screen and makes the cage escape-proof.) Provide fresh leaves for insects you collect, and give them water by sprinkling a few drops on a cotton ball that you've placed in the pan.

- Place a stalk of cut celery in a glass with a little water and about a teaspoon of food coloring. Watch what happens the next day.

- Rain gauge: Mark a tall, narrow jar, such as an olive jar, in ½-inch (1.25-cm) increments. Place funnel on top. Check daily. Keep a chart for a month. Compare your findings with the weather bureau's recorded rainfall. How close did you come?

- Hot-air balloon: Stretch the neck of a balloon over the top of a clean gallon bottle or plastic milk jug. Cool the bottle by running cold water over it for several minutes or by placing it in the refrigerator for fifteen minutes. What is in the bottle? With the balloon on the top, is there any way for what's in the bottle to get out? Is it warm or cold inside the bottle? How can you tell? Set the bottle in the sink and ask an adult to pour very hot water slowly over the outside of the cold bottle. What happens to the balloon? What would happen if the bottle were cooled again? Try it and see!

- Sponge garden: Soak a sponge in water and place it in a shallow dish. Sprinkle with alfalfa or rye grass seeds. Keep moist and watch it grow.

- Grow a crystal garden. Place four to six charcoal briquettes in an aluminum pan. In a jar, mix ¼ cup (50 g) salt, ¼ cup (60 ml) water, ¼ cup (60 ml) Mrs. Stewart's Liquid Bluing, and ¼ cup (60 ml) ammonia. Sprinkle a few drops of food coloring on the charcoal; then pour mixture over the briquettes. Make more salt mixture and add it to the garden every few days.

- Start an aquarium. Research different kinds of tropical fish on the Internet.
- Go exploring with a magnifying glass.
- Watch a sweet potato grow in a jar of water. Stick toothpicks in four sides so the bottom half is immersed in water and the top half sticks out of the jar.
- Cut off the top half of a carrot. Place it in a shallow dish of water, then watch the top sprout. You can also plant the top of a pineapple in soil.
- Start an herb garden in an egg carton and later transfer to small pots. Let your children help you season a meal with herbs they grow.
- Build a terrarium in a large jar.
- Fish for crawdads: Tie a string around a small piece of bacon and drop it in a creek. Take a bucket with you to save your catch, if you'd like.
- Make a volcano. Mound dirt 6 to 10 inches (15 to 25 cm) high and then clear a hole down the middle of it. Put 2 teaspoons baking soda in the hole. Pour in some inexpensive vinegar and watch your "eruption."

CREATIVE PLAY FOR ANY DAY

- Colorful creative salt: Add five to six drops food coloring to ½ cup (100 g) household salt. Stir well. Cook in microwave for one to two minutes or spread on waxed paper and let air-dry. Store in an airtight container. Use as you would glitter.
- Seashore chimes: Cut 12-inch (30-cm) lengths of string and tie to seashells that have holes in them. Tie the other end of each string to small pieces of driftwood. String chimes in a multistory fashion, adjusting length so the shells bump each other; hang from larger piece of driftwood. Tie on tree branch or porch beam.
- Glue art: Make squiggly designs on waxed paper with white glue. Let dry until clear, then carefully peel dried glue off the paper. Color the designs with markers. Tie with a string; hang in a window.
- Crazy putty: Combine ½ cup (118 ml) white glue and ¼ cup (60 ml) liquid starch in a bowl. Stir until blended; then knead with your hands until smooth—a couple of minutes. Stretch it like taffy or roll it into a ball and bounce it. Store it in a resealable plastic bag and it will keep for a few days.
- Festive flowers: Stack five paper cupcake liners on top of each other, then feather them out with your fingers. Use a pencil to poke two holes in the center of the stack. Insert one end of a pipe cleaner up through one hole and down the other hole, leaving one end of the pipe cleaner longer than the other.

Twist the shorter end around the longer end and extend it down to make the stem of the flower. Cut green leaves from construction paper and glue or staple them to the stem.

Paper chains: Cut colored construction paper into 1-inch-by-5-inch (2.5-cm-by-13-cm) strips. Show your child how to glue one end of the strip to the other to form a ring. Put another strip through the ring and glue the ends together. Repeat this process to make a paper chain. These chains make nice table or party decorations. Hang balloons on a chain. It is also fun to string a chain from the top of a door frame across a child's room to the opposite wall.

Handprints: Help your young child make a plaster of paris handprint. Put 1 cup (235 ml) water in a disposable bowl. Slowly add 2 cups (260 g) plaster of paris, gently allowing it to sift through your fingers. Wait about five minutes; then stir with a spoon until thickened, like soup. Pour plaster into a disposable aluminum pie pan or a heavy paper dinner plate. Wait until the plaster is almost set but still tacky to the touch. This will take about fifteen to twenty minutes, depending on the humidity and temperature. Press the child's hand with fingers spread open in the plaster to make an impression. You may want to add the year and the child's age and first name below the handprint. Wash hands, and let imprint dry completely for twenty-four hours. Remove the plaster from the pie pan or plate; then your child can paint the handprint with acrylic paints. Attach a self sticking picture hanger on the back of the plaque. Younger children may enjoy doing a footprint, too.

Lick 'em, stick 'em stamps and stickers: Mix 2 teaspoons of white liquid glue with 1 teaspoon white vinegar in a saucer. Use a small brush to paint the back of tiny pictures, pieces of artwork, or old stamps. Lay the pictures out painted-side up, making sure they don't touch each other. Let them dry completely, then lick and stick them. Children can design and color their own stickers for chore charts, school, or decorations on gift bags. You can also use the stickers to make a collage. (This recipe is also good for replacing the sticky on a stamp or envelope flap.)

Dinosaur soap bars: Stir 1 cup Ivory Snow (150 g) and ⅓ cup (80 ml) water with a spoon to create a stiff dough. Mold mixture around a small plastic toy dinosaur, forming the soap into an egg shape. Allow the soap to dry until firm. It will take about seven days, depending on the humidity and the size of the soap bar. (Use for hand washing only and not for bathing.)

Textured paint: Mix 2 teaspoons salt, 1 teaspoon liquid starch, 1 teaspoon water, and a few drops of tempera paint in a bowl. This paint makes a shiny, grainy picture. Paint with an artist-type brush on heavy paper.

- Homemade paint: Mix 1 teaspoon water and 1 teaspoon dishwashing liquid with 1 teaspoon food coloring to make vivid-colored paint. Make sure your future Rembrandt wears an apron or play clothes to do this project.

- Rock paint: Find some colored clay or crumbly rocks. Use a hammer or mortar and pestle to crush them into a powder. Turn this mixture into paint by binding it with a medium such as liquid starch, soap flakes mixed with water, cornstarch, corn syrup, or egg yolks.

- Sand pictures: On heavy cardboard, paint shapes with watered-down white glue. While glue sets, sprinkle sand over painted area. Let set, then tip to lose excess sand.

- Draw around cookie cutters on heavy paper. Color and cut out the figures. Use as bookmarks or for gift tags.

- Glue different shapes of dry macaroni to the lid of a small cardboard box. Spray-paint the box a favorite color.

- Let your child record his or her own stories on a computer.

- Refrigerator magnets: Draw a small picture of a butterfly, flower, or other object. Color the picture, cut it out, and glue it to the handle of a clip clothespin. Attach a magnet to the back of the pin with glue. Put the clothespin magnet on the refrigerator to hold artwork, cartoons, messages, or photographs.

- Paint a mural on an old sheet, using acrylic paints. Children enjoy drawing and painting animals, dinosaurs, a nature scene, their school logo, or their favorite sports teams' insignias.

- Clothing store: Collect play clothes, old hats, jewelry, scarves, ties, large paper or plastic grocery sacks, and play money. Arrange the merchandise on pretend counters; then buy and sell the items.

- Designer book covers: Use plain shelf paper or paper bags for book covers. Cut paper to fit the book. Before covering the book with the paper, dip a small brush or sponge into tempera paint and quickly dab the sponge on the bag, or flick the brush over the paper to splatter paint. (Cover work area with newspaper, wear paint clothes, and do this activity outside.) When the paint is dry, put the book cover on the book.

- Scratch designs on wax paper with a toothpick. Write a message, and give it to a friend to hold up to the light and read. Be careful not to tear the waxed paper by writing too hard.

- Snow jar: With a hole puncher, have your child cut as many holes as possible out of a piece of waxed paper. Or use 1 tablespoon glitter instead of the waxed paper circles. Put the glitter or small circles of paper into an empty baby food jar. Use waterproof glue to cement plastic animals, figures, or miniature flowers to the inside of the lid. Fill the jar with water. On the inside rim of the lid, apply a layer of waterproof glue and fasten the lid tightly. Allow it to dry, and then shake the jar.

Tin-can stilts: Use two 46-ounce (1.4-L) empty juice cans with both lids still intact. On opposite sides of the can, close to the end, punch two holes with a pointed can opener. Thread six feet of clothesline rope through the holes and tie them together with a knot. Do the same on the second can. Grip the knotted end of each rope, stand on the cans, and pull the rope up as you step. The smaller the child, the smaller the can and shorter the rope. This is a great balancing exercise for children. (This activity is recommended for children five years or older.)

Kid collage: Help your kids make collages of their lives with pictures cut from magazines. Include pictures of favorite activities, sports, foods, and animals.

Toothpick architecture: Roll modeling clay into tiny beads, about ¼ inch (6.25 mm) in diameter. Use the beads as corner joints for holding the toothpicks in place. Build houses, space stations, anything!

Rice potpourri: Add ten drops of food coloring and ten drops of scented oil to 1 cup (185 g) of uncooked long-grain rice (not instant). Put scented rice in a jar, tighten the lid, and shake well. Pour rice into a pretty bowl, and enjoy the fragrance in your room. You may want to add a few drops of oil every two weeks.

Mapping salt: Mix 1 cup (200 g) salt with 1 cup (125 g) regular white flour in a medium mixing bowl. Add ⅔ cup (160 ml) water, and stir until the mixture is as thick as icing. Add three drops or more of food coloring, depending on the shade of the color desired. You can also paint the dough with poster paint after it has dried. On a board, shape moist dough into hills, valleys, oceans, or rivers to make a topographical map or a 3-D diorama. Drying time will be determined by the thickness of the map or diorama.

Spooky sponge creatures: Cut a 4-inch (10-cm) or larger cellulose sponge (the kind that has large, irregular holes) into an animal-head shape, such as a cat, rabbit, or mouse. Cut pieces of black felt to make ears, eyes, nose, and mouth. Use a glue gun to attach face pieces to the sponge. Draw whiskers on the face with a black marker. Place a flashlight behind your animal's face and it will glow in the dark.

Box buildings: Collect empty cereal and cracker boxes, and waxed milk and cream cartons. Turn them into buildings by gluing on construction paper or brown grocery sacks cut to fit sides. Draw windows, doors, and other features. Budding architects can become city planners by drawing streets and city blocks on a large piece of paper, then placing the food-box buildings on the map. Get out a few toy cars and they can have a fun time out on the town.

- Salt sculptures: Mix together 4 cups (500 g) flour, 1½ cups (355 ml) water, and 1 cup (200 g) salt. Sculpt into shapes of animals, flowers, rockets, whatever. Bake at 350°F (180°C, or gas mark 4) for 1 hour. Cool; then paint with acrylic paint if desired.

- "Stained glass" I: Cover table or counter area with newspaper. Cut several lengths (12 to 24 inches [30 to 60 cm]) of yarn. Mix 2 tablespoons (30 ml) of white glue with 2 tablespoons (30 ml) of water in a bowl. Dip yarn pieces in glue mixture, then squeeze through fingers to remove excess glue. Press yarn pieces onto brightly colored tissue paper, creating a design. Let dry thoroughly, then trim tissue away from outside edge of yarn designs. Hang your "stained glass" designs in a window.

- "Stained Glass" II: Design stained-glass windows. Shave crayons onto waxed paper in a pattern, cover with a second sheet of waxed paper, and place inside a folded newspaper. Iron at low heat until colors are melted. Mount and display in a window.

- Family totem pole: Cut the tops off of waxed half-gallon milk cartons. Then cut 2-inch (5-cm) slits in the corners so the bottom of one container can be wedged inside the top of the container beneath it. Cover cartons with paper and decorate with designs and faces, or glue on pictures cut from magazines. Or use family photos you have duplicates of and don't mind donating to a creative cause. Put a rock or weight in the bottom carton for stability, then stack others on top.

- Twig architecture: Have your child collect small twigs and organize them by size. Start a twig house by inserting two upright twigs into the ground diagonally at each corner, then lay horizontal twigs, log-cabin-style, to build walls. Place leaves and plant stalks across the top of twig structures to make thatched roofs. Build a fence and even an entire village.

- Mud-brick architecture: Mix water in soil until texture is like dough. (If soil is sandy, add one part flour to four parts soil.) Shape into rectangles; let set until dry. Use a wet table knife to cut various-size bricks. Stack bricks, spreading a fresh batch of mud as mortar between layers. Smooth excess with a plastic knife. Build houses, walls, even cities!

- Rice art: Draw a simple picture on cardboard. In butter tubs, use food coloring to dye rice different colors. Dip a toothpick in white glue, then pick up one grain of rice. Dip it into the glue again and place the rice grain on the picture. When the picture is completely covered with rice, brush a coat of glue over entire surface. It will dry clear.

- Homemade paste: Mix ½ cup (115 g) flour with ½ cup (120 ml) water until smooth. Store in covered container. For more durable paste, add ½ cup (115 g) flour to 1 cup (240 ml) boiling water. Stir over low heat until thick and shiny.

- Play dough: Mix 2 cups (250 g) flour, 1 cup (200 g) salt, 4 teaspoons cream of tartar, 2 cups (475 ml) water, 2 tablespoons (30 ml) salad oil, and food coloring. Stir ingredients together, then cook in a saucepan over medium heat until dough follows spoon and leaves the side of the pan. Cool and knead. Store in airtight container.

- Kool-Aid dough: Mix 1 cup (125 g) sifted flour, ½ cup (100 g) salt, 3 tablespoons (45 ml) oil, and 1 small package of Kool-Aid or other unsweetened powdered drink. Add 1 cup (235 ml) boiling water. Stir ingredients together, then knead mixture until it forms a soft dough.

- Creative clay: In medium pan, mix 1 cup (130 g) cornstarch and 2 cups (440 g) baking soda. Add 1¼ cups (295 ml) cold water and stir over medium heat until mixture has the consistency of mashed potatoes. Remove from pan, and cover with damp cloth until cool enough to knead. Store in airtight container. This clay makes great Christmas ornaments, pottery, or sculptures. It works best if dried at room temperature for three days but can be dried in a 200°F (95°C) oven for one to three hours, depending on the thickness of the clay piece.

- Baker's clay: Mix 2 cups (250 g) white flour and ½ cup (100 g) table salt in a bowl. Add ½ cup (120 ml) water and stir for a few minutes. Slowly add ¼ cup (60 ml) water while turning dough in bowl. Form dough into a ball. Knead for five minutes. Shape dough into desired shapes, adding a little water to join pieces together. Use cookie cutters for preschoolers. Bake your creations at 250°F (120°C, or gas mark ½) for fifteen to thirty minutes, until hard. Time will vary according to thickness of dough. Let cool completely. Dough can be painted with acrylic paints.

- Paint with a plastic straw by dipping one end of it into tempera or poster paint. Hold the straw over a piece of paper and blow. Use a different straw for each color of paint. This is a good outside activity.

- Sunshine prints: Place ferns, flowers, or leaves on colored construction paper in the sun. Leave outside for a day. Outlines of the plants will be printed on the paper.

- Build a fort with scrap wood.

"Spend the afternoon. You can't take it with you."
—Annie Dillard

- Ask an interior designer for an old wallpaper book. Cut out circles, rectangles, squares, triangles, or other creative shapes. Glue them on construction paper to make all kinds of interesting pictures.

- Refurbish an old skateboard by painting it, then adding decals and new accessories.

- Sand-paint an American flag for the Fourth of July. You will need 4 cups white sand. Mix one-third of it with 1½ tablespoons dry red tempera paint. Mix another third with 1½ tablespoons dry blue paint, and leave the remaining sand white. Draw a flag design on sturdy cardboard. Working with one color at a time, spread glue over the marked-off design, sprinkle the colored sand over it, let dry, then shake off extra sand. Repeat the process with the other colors. When dry, seal with clear plastic spray.

- Soapy finger paint: Whip 1 cup soap flakes with ½ cup (120 ml) water. Tint with food coloring or dry tempera. Paint on white shelf paper or waxed paper.

- Homemade finger paint: Mix 2 cups (250 g) flour with 2 teaspoons salt. Add 2½ cups (590 ml) cold water. Stir until smooth. Gradually add this mixture to 2 cups (475 ml) boiling water. Boil until smooth and thick. Add food coloring; then stir until smooth.

- Home-style paint roller: Cut a cardboard wrapping paper tube to the length of a paint roller. Glue pieces of yarn or pipe cleaners in designs around the tube. Slip the tube over a paint roller and roll it first in paint, then over a large piece of paper to make all kinds of interesting patterns.

- Giant paint pen: Pry the top off a roll-on deodorant bottle and wash it out. Fill it with tempera or poster paint and snap top back on. You'll have a giant roller pen!

- Raindrop art: Fill empty saltshakers or spice bottles with dry tempera paint. Sprinkle paint on poster board. Use a spray bottle to squirt water on the picture. Let it dry, then shake off excess paint powder.

- Doodle paint: Mix ½ cup each salt (100 g), water (120 ml), and flour (65 g) with 1 tablespoon cornstarch and eight drops food coloring. Stir well. Poor into a plastic squeeze bottle (an empty mustard or ketchup bottle works well). Squeeze paint onto large pieces of poster board.

- Chalk paint: Dissolve 6 tablespoons (75 g) sugar in ¼ cup (60 ml) water. Soak chalk ten minutes. Draw on colored paper with wet chalk.

- Finger paint with shaving cream on colored construction paper.

- Make mud pies or mud stew with twigs, rocks, and acorns.

- Make inkblot animals, using an ink pad, black pen, and paper. Press your index finger on an ink pad and then on the paper. Use a pen to draw eyes, ears, tails, and wings, and create miniature animals. (Be careful; it will permanently stain clothes! Wash hands immediately afterward.)

- Make musical instruments. Put dry rice between two paper plates and tape them together to make a shaker. Cover one end of a paper towel tube with paper. Poke holes in the tube, then hum through the open end. This makes a great horn. Wrap tissue or waxed paper around a comb and hum into it for a neat kazoo.

- Write crazy commercials and perform them for each other.

- Plan a neighborhood talent show. Serve homemade ice cream.

- Make sock puppets from old socks, extra buttons, and yarn.

- Create your own slide show. Use old, exposed slides that no one cares about. Rub off the photograph on the slide with a cotton swab dipped in household bleach. The slide will turn blue at first but will become clear with more rubbing. Draw little pictures on the slide with colored marker pens.

- Print on paper by dipping the following objects in tempera paint: a potato cut in half with a design carved in the raw end, a cork, a bottle cap, or a spool.

- Make a bird feeder by rolling a pinecone in peanut butter, then in birdseed. Hang from a tree with string.

- Make "funny faces" makeup by mixing cold cream with food coloring. (Wash your face with liquid facial cleanser and wipe dry before painting. This makes cleanup easier.)

- Tennis-ball puppets: Cut a slit across an old tennis ball. Outline the slit with a red marker for a mouth. Draw a nose and eyes and glue yarn on for hair. Squeeze the back of the ball to make the puppet talk.

- Make finger puppets from toilet paper tubes. Draw faces and glue yarn on for hair. Cover a table with a sheet for a puppet theater.

WEARABLE ART

- Designer apparel: Use acrylic paints, paint pens, or puff paint (which can be purchased at craft stores and makes puffy figures or designs) to draw decorative designs on boxer shorts, ribbons, T-shirts, and sweats.

- Make quick costumes from old pillowcases. Help your child cut a hole for the neck and arms. Use markers, acrylic paints, scrap fringe or lace to decorate the pillowcase. Ribbon or heavy yarn can be used for a belt. Pretend characters are unlimited.

- Splatter acrylic paint on an old pair of white tennis shoes. Draw designs on shoelaces with paint pens.

- Tie-dye a T-shirt (100 percent cotton works best). Gather a small wad of the T-shirt in your hand, then tightly wrap a rubber band around the gathered fabric. Repeat this procedure all over the T-shirt. Follow directions carefully on the fabric dye package. After the shirt is dyed, cut off the rubber bands before drying. Interesting white designs will now be wherever the rubber bands held the fabric together.

- Leaf crown: Make a chain of large, flat leaves by piercing the stem of one leaf into another. Pull the stem through as far as it will go. The next leaf will hide the stem. Continue until your chain is long enough to go around your head. Make a circle by poking the last stem into the first.

- Crazy caps: Decorate old baseball caps by gluing on beads, ribbons, sequins, feathers, fabric scraps, pipe cleaners, buttons, artificial flowers, or anything else on hand. Have a contest for the craziest cap creation.

- Salt beads: Mix 2 cups (400 g) salt and 1 cup (125 g) flour with enough water to make a doughy mixture. Form bead-size balls and make a hole through the center of each with a toothpick. Or cover 1-inch (2.5-cm) lengths of straws with dough to make larger beads. Let dry; then paint beads with tempera or acrylic paints in bright colors. String them into necklaces or bracelets.

- Mask mania: Cut empty gallon-size plastic containers in half, then cut out openings for eyes, nose, and mouth. Glue yarn for hair, and twirl pipe cleaners for side ringlets. Glue cutout felt shapes for mustache and eyebrows. Use sequins, feathers, and glue for an exotic look. Poke a hole in each side of the container and then tie ribbons or a piece of elastic string to hold masks in place.

- Pasta gems: Mix 1 tablespoon (15 ml) food coloring with 2 tablespoons (30 ml) rubbing alcohol. Make several different colors. Stir macaroni into the colored solutions and spread on a newspaper to dry. String on a shoelace for bracelets or necklaces.

- Sunflower-seed necklaces: Soak seeds in warm water for one hour. Use dental floss and an embroidery needle to string the seeds. Let necklace dry before wearing.

- Sponge paint: Cut out various shapes or designs from sponges. Press them in paint and use them to decorate paper, T-shirts, hats, whatever!

MORE WAYS TO MAKE YOUR OWN FUN AND GAMES

- Batting practice: Drill a hole through the center of a baseball. Thread a long piece of rope through the hole and knot it. Tie the other end of the rope to a tree limb so that the ball hangs down to about the level of your child's waist. Now when you practice swinging and hit the ball, it will always come back.

- Play parachutes: Cut four 18-inch (45-cm) lengths of sturdy string. Tie one end of string to each corner of a man's handkerchief. Thread the other end of all four strings through an empty thread spool and tie them to a paper clip. Wrap the strings and handkerchief around the spool. Toss up in the air, and the parachutes will unfold and billow out as they fall.

- Set up an art gallery. Cut a piece of clothesline to stretch across one wall of a child's bedroom. Tie knotted loops at each end of the line, then mount cup hooks at both ends of the wall, so that the pictures are at the child's eye level. Attach the clothesline loops to the hooks, and hang great works of art with clothespins.

- Bicycle parade: Round up the neighborhood kids (and their parents) and help them decorate their bikes and trikes with red, white, and blue streamers, ribbons, flowers, pinwheels, balloons, and homemade cardboard license plates. Use clothespins to secure playing cards to the spokes of the wheels to make a roaring "engine" noise. It's a great way to kick off the Fourth of July.

- Write a play, design costumes, and stage a performance.

- Write a script and film your own movie or make your own music video.

- Make maracas by covering old light bulbs with at least three or four layers of papier-mâché. When dry, very gently tap each one to break the bulb inside. Be careful not to make a hole so glass can escape. Paint your maracas with festive colors and dance around the house!

- Make dolls from thread spools. Use markers to make faces; glue on yarn for hair, and pieces of colored paper or fabric scraps for clothes.

- Paint rocks with tempera paint.

- Create a mosaic by cutting construction paper into zillions of small pieces and gluing them to a sheet of paper to create patterns or scenes.

- Check out classic stories on CDs or cassette tapes from the library.

- Write and illustrate your own picture storybook. Make up adventure or mystery stories and write them on a computer or in a blank book.

- Visit the Web site of states you would like to visit and collect information about fun things to do and interesting places to go on vacation.

- Design your own letterhead.

- Buy inexpensive plastic cups or mugs. Decorate and personalize with paint pens.

- Make a scrapbook of papers, pictures, and reports from the previous school year.

- Create a My Summer Notebook. Draw pictures and write about what you do each week.

- Creative bubbles: Mix together equal amounts of dishwashing liquid, water, and glycerin. (You can buy glycerin at any pharmacy. It makes the bubbles last longer.) Put the solution in a wide pan, like a cake pan, and use different things from around the house as wands, such as a clean flyswatter and a slotted spatula.

- Ice sculpture: For birthdays, holidays, and just for fun, make a colored ice sculpture as a centerpiece for the table. Fill gelatin or animal-shaped molds with water tinted with food coloring, freeze, and unmold onto a nice platter. Garnish the sculpture with whatever berries, flowers, or greens you have in your yard. You can also freeze juices such as apple or grape in a mold and put them in the punch bowl for a festive touch.

- Spuzzles: Wash and dry some wooden ice-cream sticks; lay them beside each other. Secure a piece of tape across all the sticks. Turn them over and draw a picture with markers. Remove the tape, then mix up the sticks, and put the picture together.

- Shiny pennies: Kids love to make pennies look like new. Mix 4 tablespoons (60 ml) vinegar and 1 teaspoon salt in a small bowl. Drop pennies into the solution. If the pennies don't instantly become clean, stir them for a minute with a wooden spoon, then polish them with a soft cloth and a drop of vegetable oil to make them shine.

- Design a do-it-yourself strobe light. Drill or cut a 2-inch (5-cm) hole in an old LP record. Remove the blade from an old fan and mount the record in its place. Turn fan on low and place flashlight behind it in a dark room.

- Turn old tires into creative fun. Make a tire swing or a target for a football or Frisbee.

- Use a long wrapping paper tube to make a slide for small cars, balls, or other toys.

- Create a collage by gluing different kinds of beans, cereal, colored toothpicks, dry rice, foil, macaroni, or raisins onto cardboard.

- Build a dollhouse by stacking five shoe boxes or cardboard boxes to resemble a two-story house with a garage. Paint and decorate. Create furniture by covering smaller boxes with fabric or contact paper.

- Make flavored toothpicks with peppermint or cinnamon oil, which you can buy at your local pharmacy.

- Build a model plane or car from a kit.

- Cut a large picture from a magazine, such as an animal, car, or face. Cut the picture down the middle and glue one half of it on white paper. Now draw the other half of the picture.

- Collect as many dominos as you can. Stack them in a long design just far enough apart that when you push one, the others will fall down consecutively.

- Buy used small appliances at a secondhand store. Take them apart and put them back together.

- Write a letter to the president. Ask him to send you a book about the White House.

- Spray pinecones with gold paint. Use a hot glue gun (a wonderful investment) to attach a Christmas ornament hook.

- Learn to juggle using rubber balls or homemade beanbags.

- Make a giant slingshot for water balloons in the backyard. Secure two 4-foot (1.2-m) wood or metal poles in the ground about 4 feet (1.2 m) apart. Drill two holes in the opposite sides of the wide mouth of a plastic or tin funnel. Cut rubber tubing into two pieces, 3 feet (1 m) long and 1½ inches (3.75 cm) wide. The tubing can be purchased from a service station or tire store. Attach first strip to one funnel hole and pole. Attach the other piece of tubing to the opposite funnel hole and pole. Fill balloons with water, hold against the wide end of the funnel, pull back, and fire away at whatever target you choose!

- Build a catapult with rubber bands and Tinkertoys or scrap wood. Bombard targets with flying objects.

- Play marbles. Draw a circle on the ground and put several marbles in the middle of it. Shoot a marble from outside the circle and see how many others you can knock out.

- Pressed flowers: Place flowers, leaves, or ferns between sheets of paper towels. Put several heavy books over the paper towels. Allow thin flowers to dry about five days; thick flowers will take up to a month. When flowers are dry, cut clear Con-Tact paper in a rectangle to fit the flowers. Remove backing from Con-Tact paper, and put flowers on the sticky side. Cut a second piece of clear Con-Tact paper the same size, and place the sticky side over the flowers. Tape the flower print to a window or back it with construction paper.

- Glue interesting fabric to the cover of a notebook. Use it to record addresses, goals, and prayers. Make a pocket in it to save important papers or coupons.

- Make musical bottles. Line up an assortment of empty bottles in various sizes and shapes, add water, and blow gently across the top. By adding or pouring out water, you can change the pitch. See if you can play a tune.
- Take a walk with a memento bag and collect interesting leaves, rocks, or junk you find along the way. Mount your finds on cardboard, and hang it in a prominent spot.
- Learn calligraphy.
- Create your own crossword puzzles.
- Learn the art of wood carving.
- Call your local hospital or YMCA to find out about first-aid, CPR, or babysitting classes.

FUN FIELD TRIPS

- Visit the fire station.
- Go to the post office. Let your children send letters to themselves and then watch for the mail carrier the next day.
- Take a nature walk. Collect ferns, flowers, leaves, and rocks to make a centerpiece for the dinner table. Study birds, leaves, and wildflowers. Try to identify them. Make a nature book of the things you've studied.
- Find a construction site and watch the trucks and tractors.
- Arrange for a tour of the police station.
- Visit a bakery and ask the bakers to show you how they decorate cakes or prepare the pastries for baking.
- Go to a dairy farm.
- Make an appointment to see a newspaper—or magazine—printing plant.
- Check an automobile-tour guidebook for local historical sights and go visit them.
- Attend a county courthouse or city-council session. Visit the mayor's office. (With these ideas, be sure to call ahead to learn hours and dates of operation and whether an appointment is necessary.)
- Tour a factory or large business in your community.
- Go to the top of the tallest building in your area. See what landmarks you can spot.
- Take part in a religious service of a group different from your own.
- Go shopping at a flea market. Look for items to add to a collection, used toys or sports equipment, or a piece of furniture for your room.

- Visit a farm where you can pick your own fruit or berries; then head home and make jam or cobbler.

- Take a camera scavenger hunt. Decide on a theme-nature, architecture, or sports, for example. Go on an adventure and find objects that illustrate your area of interest. Photograph them. Make an album of your outing.

- Have a transportation celebration day. Take a ride on a bus, train, or subway. Go for a long drive or bike ride. Go to an airport and watch the planes take off and land. Record your family's experiences, keeping a travel journal about where you went and what you saw along the way. At dinner tell everyone about which mode of transportation you liked best-and why.

- Find out if you can visit a local TV or radio station and watch a broadcast.

- See if there is a candy factory near you where you can watch chocolate being melted, molded, foiled, packed, and shipped.

- Find out from your state's Fisheries and Wildlife Commission where fish hatcheries are located near your home, and visit one.

- Visit a museum. Before taking the kids, go to the museum and pick up informational brochures or visit the museum's Web site. When you go on your outing, send the children on a museum scavenger hunt by giving them a list of exhibits or works of art to identify.

BIG FUN FOR SMALL FRIES

- Make boats to float. Take a 2-inch (5-cm) cork and slit one end. Color a sail-shaped piece of paper with crayons to waterproof it, then insert it into the slit. Sail it in the bathtub, sink, or a small backyard pool.

- Make a design with a hole punch in a paper plate. Your child can string a shoelace through the holes.

- Pan for gold: Bury pennies in a sand box. Your kids can search for the pennies, using plastic colanders or sieves.

- Matching numbers: Cut the numbered squares from an old calendar. Have your child match the numbered pieces to the numbers on the whole calendar page, line the numbered squares in the correct sequence, or use them to play addition or subtraction.

- Buy sample carpet squares at a flooring store for a nominal price. Children enjoy jumping from one square to another. Put a carpet square under the dining room or kitchen table for a special place to sit and read books or have a snack. Play circus animal trainer: line up stuffed animals on carpet squares.

- Flannel-board stories: Cover a 2-by-3-foot (60-by-90-cm) piece of cardboard with plain white or light blue flannel for a storyboard. Your child can cut out animals, people, or objects from catalogs or magazines and glue flannel on the back of them. You can also use white interfacing, available at fabric stores, and trace animals, characters, or objects from favorite storybooks or from coloring books. Color the interfacing characters with crayons. Make up flannel-board figures for favorite stories, and keep the figures and stories in a large envelope. Storytelling is an excellent way to help children develop language skills.

- Tricycle traffic: Construct road signs out of poster board and attach them to sticks or dowel rods. Plant the signs in cans with dirt so they will stand up straight. Design a highway on the sidewalk or patio with masking tape. Position road signs along the marked roadways. One child can pretend to be the policeman and direct traffic, while the other children ride tricycles or wheeled toys.

- Animal safari: Hide your preschooler's stuffed animals around the house-under the bed, peeking around a chest, inside a cabinet or in a closet. Turn off all the lights and use a flashlight to go on a safari to capture the animals.

- Pack an old suitcase with clothes and costume jewelry for dress-up.

- Hide a kitchen timer and have your child search for it by listening for its ticking sound.

- Punch holes in the bottom of an oatmeal or shoe box. Shine a flashlight in the box toward the ceiling in a darkened room. (This is excellent for toddlers who resist nap times.)

- Play with a magnet. Show your child what it will and will not pick up. Make a fishing pole with a stick and string. Tie a magnet on the end. Have your child fish for paper clips.

- Have a washday for doll clothes. Fill a tub or large basin with soapy water, and wash, rinse, and hang the clothes out to dry.

- On a warm, rainy day, stage boat races in the gutter or stomp through puddles.

- Tape different-colored paper circles to the inside of each cup in a muffin tin. Cut other paper circles in the same colors. Have your child match the circles with those in the muffin tin.

- Conduct a neighborhood tricycle wash.

- Teach kids to make paper-clip chains.

- Make real-people puppets by cutting out photos of family members and friends. Glue to Popsicle sticks or tongue depressors.

- Create pictures by pressing assorted lengths of yarn on coarse sandpaper. You can pull off the yarn and start all over again.

- Make "my shadow" pictures. Have your children lie down on a large piece of cardboard. Trace around their entire bodies, then cut out the figures. Let them color in the features and dress the figures in their own clothes.

- Make a pipe-cleaner floral arrangement. Line a small plastic strawberry basket with enough colored tissue paper so the paper sticks up 3 to 4 inches (7.5 to 10 cm) above the top. Cut a ½-inch- (1.25-cm-) thick piece of Styrofoam to fit snugly inside. Draw and cut various flower shapes out of construction paper. Glue flowers to pipe-cleaner stems, then insert into Styrofoam.

- Make paper airplanes. See which one can fly the farthest and perform the best aerobatics.

- Make up fun jingles to recite when jumping rope.

- Make a homemade piñata. Tape boxes together to make a real or imaginary animal figure (place toys and candies inside). Decorate by gluing on bits of crepe paper, feathers, or leaves; hang with string from a tree. Let kids take turns trying to break it open.

23 THINGS TO DO WITH A BIG BOX

1. Create a puppet theater. Cut an opening in the front of the box and another in the back for a door. Make a curtain out of an old sheet or towel. On with the show!

2. Put on a backyard carnival. Build booths from refrigerator boxes. Have face-painting and pie-throwing (whipped cream on paper plates) contests. Make a ring toss using old coat hangers as the rings and soda-pop bottles as the targets. Design a beanbag toss. Sell tickets to the neighborhood kids and give out small prizes.

3. Make pup tents. Cut off the bottom and top off a large appliance box. Cut down the center of one side and fold into a triangle; tape the two cut pieces together to make the floor. Spray-paint the tent to add color.

4. Design and build a puppy condo as a summer home for your dog.

I've spent a lot on games and toys
It's a parent's paradox
My children always have more fun
With a big old cardboard box.

5. Construct a castle from a carton, cutting notches along the top like a castle wall. At the bottom, create a door that opens like a drawbridge.

6. Make a Western town for your cowboys out of appliance boxes of various sizes. Make a church, jail, barbershop, general store, opera house, or red barn.

7. Make a ticket booth out of a refrigerator box for your backyard carnivals, plays, and puppet shows.

8. Backyard obstacle course. Create an obstacle course where your kids can crawl under lawn chairs or through tunnels made from large boxes, walk or hop along a curvy garden hose, and dodge an oscillating sprinkler. Make it a little more difficult each time they do it by having each child balance a Ping-Pong ball on a paper plate or try to get through the course blindfolded.

9. Invent a model of a car or truck, using cardboard boxes and paint.

10. Flatten a mattress box to make a city or airport for small cars or planes.

11. Make a lemonade stand. Turn the box topside-down to make a table, then cut away the unnecessary pieces or let them spread out on the ground.

12. Cut a large appliance box so it can be laid flat. Paint a giant mural on it with tempera paint.

13. Create a submarine. Cut portholes and make a periscope from a cardboard tube.

14. Make a rocket from a tall refrigerator carton.

15. Create a portrait screen. Paint characters or animals on a tall box. Cut holes where the characters' faces should be for the kids to stick their faces through. Take a snapshot of them.

16. Construct a zoo. Put stuffed animals in box cages.

17. Build a train by connecting three medium-size boxes. Decorate and take dolls, stuffed animals, and toys for a ride.

18. Connect two large boxes to make a two-room playhouse. Have your child play interior designer and decorate as fancy as he or she wants.

19. Make a reading hideout. Add lots of pillows and a "do not disturb" sign.

20. Design a robot using different-sized boxes and cardboard tubes for legs and arms. Use buttons, felt, ribbon, and rickrack for features.

21. Tape large boxes together to make a tunnel.

22. Make a costume from an open-ended box. Cut holes for head and arms, then decorate with crayons or markers.

23. Design an airplane or spaceship from a big box. Draw a control panel and suggest the kids pretend they are flying to a fun place.

QUALITY TIME TOGETHER

- As a family, work and frame a jigsaw puzzle each summer. Hang it in a child's room or game room. Be sure to write the date on the back.

- Make a family member feel special. Decorate his or her room with balloons, crepe paper, and signs.

- Fly kites as a family.

 "Ah! There's nothing like staying home for real comfort." —Jane Austen

- Have the children record interesting sounds in the neighborhood on a tape recorder. Ask them to play it back to you and have you guess the sounds.

- Have a family watercolor night. Each person paints his or her favorite vacation spot or place the family has gone on an outing.

- Cloud watching: Lie on a blanket in the backyard with your child. Look at the clouds and see if you can pick out the shapes of animals, faces, or objects.

- Treasure hunt: Post clues such as pictures, words, or silly rhymes to direct your kids from one location to another until they find the treasure. Use picture clues for preschoolers, and let them hunt for their afternoon snack. Your kids will enjoy hunting for a birthday gift, money for an ice cream cone, coupons for miniature golf, or other special treats.

- Bigger and better: Divide into two or more teams of two to eight players. Give each team a penny. Set a time limit for forty-five minutes, then send the kids into the neighborhood to ask neighbors if they'll give them an item in exchange for the penny. The kids then take the item they received to a second house, and ask if they'll give them something bigger and better in trade. The team that comes home with the biggest and best item wins. Don't be surprised if they return home with some big white elephants.

- Babysitting kit: Make up a box filled with creative projects for little ones. Include some of the easy crafts from this book. (Young people can take this kit with them when they babysit.)

- Invent a new flavor of ice cream. Begin with a plain flavor and add nuts, chocolate chips, crumbled candy bars, crushed cookies, chocolate-coated raisins, candies, or peanut butter. Brainstorm together about what you'll call it.

- Save coins in a jar. Count and roll them. Then use the money at the end of the summer for a family outing to the ice-cream parlor.

- Make a "because we love you" box for a family member who has had a hard week. Write notes and buy small, inexpensive gifts.

- Cook breakfast at a park. Let your kids help as much as possible.

- Make a family tree. See how far back you can trace your ancestry.

- Start a lunch club for your daughter's friends. Take turns preparing lunch with other moms and rotate homes. Concentrate on manners, menu planning, and table setting.

- Summer is a great time to develop good personal hygiene grooming rituals in your preteens. They're old enough to understand that appearance and personal habits tell others a lot about how they feel about themselves. Teach your children to make the most of the equipment God has given them by learning to take good care of their skin, hair, and bodies. Make a personal hygiene drawer or basket for each of them.

- Watch the stars. Lie on a blanket in the backyard with an astronomy chart and flashlight.

- Play charades.

- Picnic at a different park each week.

- Go exploring one afternoon on the back roads; see what you can discover. Take along a snack.

- Make a family video of your summer. Tape fun things each week.

- Talk about a different culture or country one night a week. Eat the food of that country.

- Sock wars: Roll socks into balls and clear one room of all breakable items. Divide into two teams, decide on boundary lines, and fire. When our boys were young, we played the theme music from Star Wars during the battle.

- Learn a new vocabulary word each day at a family meal. Conduct a family vocabulary contest.

- Make plans for Dad to go on a date with a daughter or for Mom to go on a date with a son. Dress up and go to a favorite restaurant. You can also have a "just the boys" or "just the girls" night out.

- Play a family game of basketball, kick ball, or softball.

- Take a bike hike to an interesting picnic spot.

- Teach your kids to skip rocks on a lake.

- Make a family treasure chest. Decorate a plastic bin or a dress or suit box with colorful paper or paint, glitter, and ribbon. Use the box to store children's art-work, awards, memorabilia from a fun outing, report cards, and school pictures. Once a year, look into the box together and reminisce about those special events.

- Have an ongoing tournament with the following favorite family games: chess, Sorry!, Global Pursuit, Junior Trivia, Monopoly, Scrabble, Tile Rummy, USA Trivia, Yahtzee, Pictionary.

- Check with a community college for summer continuing education classes that children can attend with you. Courses in art, computer, drama, sports, dog obedience, floral design, foreign language, or speed reading would be fun to do together.

- Discuss a current event each night at dinner.

- Host a neighborhood scavenger hunt.

- Invite families over for a build-your-own-banana-split party. Ask each family to bring a favorite topping to share.

- Organize an all-neighborhood garage sale.

- Help the children collect unwanted items from neighbors and give them to charitable organizations.

- Visit a nursing home with your children. Play games with the residents.

- Together, write a family newsletter and e-mail or mail it to relatives. Include a gossip column (who made the honor roll, who has a new boyfriend, who bought a new car), an article on family genealogy, a family trivia quiz, or a calendar of family events.

- Choose parts and read a play aloud as a family.

- Have a family meeting and make a list of the positive qualities of each member. This is a great self-esteem builder!

- Write and perform a family play. Make a videotape and send it to Grandma and Grandpa.

- Have a smile contest. See who has the biggest smile; measure them with a ruler.

- Every week, post brainteasers, riddles, and word puzzles in a central location. The first one to tell Mom the right answer wins. Announce the winner at dinner on Saturday night.

- Take a lot of family pictures-the crazier the pose, the better. Fill family albums with photos and write in captions or notes of interest.

- Make up a family trivia game. Write questions on the front of index cards and the answers on the back. Stack the cards in a pile and let family members take turns drawing. If the question is answered correctly, the player keeps the card. The person with the most cards wins. Here are some ideas for questions:

⊚ Where did Mom and Dad go on their first date?

⊚ What was James's first word?

⊚ What car was Kristen driving when she passed her driver's test?

⊚ On what vacation did John learn to snap his fingers?

💡 Turn an ordinary walk to the park into an alphabet hunt. On a pad, list all of the letters of the alphabet. While you're walking, check off the letters when you spot something that starts with the letter you're looking for.

💡 Build a tree house together.

💡 Have a family car wash. Wear bathing suits and be ready for sponge fights and water-squirt wars.

💡 Does an elderly couple or widow live in your neighborhood? Ask if your family can clean out the garage, move heavy objects, mow the lawn, wash the windows, or paint a room or the outside of the house for them.

💡 Family silhouettes: Use a bright lamp to project the head profile of each family member on a blank wall. Tape a piece of construction paper to the wall and trace the silhouette. Cut it out and glue it on paper of a contrasting color.

💡 Have a progressive dinner with two other families. Eat salad at one home, the main course at the next, and have dessert at the last, along with a big game of hide-and-seek, kick ball, or volleyball.

💡 Devise your own family secret code, with numbers representing letters. Communicate by sending one another coded messages.

💡 Teach your children to yo-yo.

💡 Plant and work a garden together. Check with your local seed store for what kind of vegetables, fruits, and flowers grow easily in your area. Or start an herb garden in small pots. Have your children check each day for growth.

💡 Set up a miniature golf course in your backyard (use croquet mallets and balls or a plastic baseball bat and ball to play the course). Use old boards propped on a brick or log to make an incline to go up and over. Make a tunnel for the ball to go through from a piece of hollow log or PVC pipe. Make an obstacle course from empty paint cans set in rows. Use an old piece of gutter as a trough for the ball to pass through. (Drive small stakes on each side to hold the trough upright.) Mark your "holes" with flags made from construction paper and sticks.

💡 Have walnut races. Clean out walnut shell halves and turn the shells into animals, using felt-tip markers, glue, construction paper, feathers, cotton, and tiny bits of fabric scraps. Line up the animals on a card table, each inverted over a marble and held back by a yardstick. Gently tip the table and remove the yardstick. See which animal wins.

- Help your child start a collection. When deciding what to collect, think about interests you and your child share, as well as the cost of the items and how much space you have for storage. Some ideas to consider: autographs, sports cards, snow globes, bells, postcards, stamps, baseball caps, marbles, fossils, buttons, shells, feathers, piggy banks.

- Build miniature houses with playing cards.

- Let the kids plan menus and shop for groceries with a budgeted amount of money.

- Make a homemade memory game by cutting 8-inch (20-cm) squares out of poster board. Glue matching pairs of pictures (two balls, boys, girls, horses, etc.) from cereal boxes or magazines on the cards. Turn them facedown, choose one card at a time, and ask your child to identify the matching pictures when they come up.

- Make place mats by covering kids' art work with clear Con-Tact paper.

- Make superhero capes for stuffed animals with scraps of fabric. When your kids see them, they'll want capes too!

- When the family goes to sports events, make a special entertainment bag for younger children. Fill it with books, cars, crayons, notepad, and plastic people.

- Invite your child's teacher over for dinner to say "thank you" for a good year.

- Buy or check out a library book on cake decorating and learn with your kids.

- Write secret messages to each other using white crayon on white paper. To decipher the message, tell the person to paint the paper with watercolors, and the message will appear.

- Bake brownies with your children and send the goodies to a friend they met at camp or to one who moved away from your neighborhood.

- With your children, bake a sheet cake for the Fourth of July. Ice it like an American flag.

- Start a recipe file for your teenage son or daughter.

- Let a professional cosmetologist show your daughter how to apply just enough makeup to bring out her natural beauty.

- Teach cross-stitching by using simple patterns.

- Mount your children's pictures, display them in a special place, and host an art show for Dad or Grandma.

- Make a greeting-card scrapbook. Have the children write a few sentences on what their birthdays, Father's Day, Mother's Day, or other special occasions mean to them. Paste essays in the book beside the appropriate cards. Continue the collection throughout the years.

CHAPTER NINE

Family Fun for All

"I pray you . . . your play needs no excuse.
Never excuse. . . ." —William Shakespeare

OUR CHILDREN'S MINDS ARE LIKE VIDEO CAMERAS, constantly recording every thing they see, hear, and do. Who's to know which memories will be edited out or recorded over? And which will become part of their permanent archives? We have the privilege of choosing to include fun in our everyday family lives so the chances are better that their memories will be good ones.

Take advantage of these long summer days and mellow summer nights. And remember, not every memory maker has to be a huge undertaking. All you need is a can-do attitude! Here are some fun ideas for your family to try.

ENJOY THE GREAT OUTDOORS. Camping out at a state or national park or simply pitching a tent in your own backyard can be a great adventure. Try to pitch your tent on flat ground and facing east so the first rays of sunshine will bring warmth the next morning. It's also fun to hang a flag or pennant at your campsite. (You can make a flag from a rectangular piece of sturdy cloth, tacked to a pole.) Whether you're camping out or just having a late-night adventure, try some of these activities.

☀ Create your own constellations. What do you see in the sky in the way of people, animals, and common objects? Name them. Some of ours have been the Big Spatula, Nana's Coffee Cup, and Celestial Seesaw.

Foil Dinners over a Campfire

Tear off a 20-inch (50-cm) length of heavy-duty aluminum foil. Grease one side with butter or margarine. Break up ¼ pound (115 g) ground beef or turkey into small chunks, and place it on greased foil. Layer thinly sliced potatoes and carrots on the meat. Sprinkle with dry onion soup mix, and top with three pats of butter. Fold foil over the food and secure tightly, leaving room for air to circulate within the packet. Then fold over each end tightly so the juices won't run out. Place the foil packet directly on hot coals for 10 minutes. Turn the packet over carefully, and cook for another 10 minutes. Carefully unfold the foil, letting the steam escape, and eat right out of it. Make one for each person in your family.

☀ Tell a continuing story—an exciting drama or a hilarious comedy. One family member starts the story, and each person adds more to the adventure.

☀ Make up animal or adventure stories that feature your children as the main characters.

☀ Use this opportunity to get to know each other better. Ask questions like: What do you feel you're good at? What do you wish you were better at? What do you wish you could do that you don't know how to do? What's your favorite time of day? Why? What do you like to do with the family? If you could travel anyplace in the world, where would you go?

☀ Sing songs around a campfire.

☀ Catch fireflies in a jar and watch them light up. Try to time the intervals between flashes. Notice the variations in color.

☀ Listen for nocturnal animals; see how many you can identify. You don't need to be near a wilderness area to hear a number of different animals that hunt for food when the sun goes down. Raccoons, skunks, opossums, and mice are among the mammals that live near people.

☀ Go on a walk with a flashlight and look for the opening of night-blooming flowers such as moonflowers, evening primrose, datura, and evening-scented stock.

TAKE PLENTY OF PICNICS. Keep a picnic basket and cooler easily accessible, and an extra bag of ice in the freezer for impromptu outings.

Use this Picnic Checklist to make sure you're ready for food and fun in the outdoors.

- ☐ Food and condiments
- ☐ Beverages
- ☐ Water
- ☐ Ice
- ☐ Paper plates
- ☐ Paper cups
- ☐ Eating utensils
- ☐ Serving utensils
- ☐ Napkins
- ☐ Tablecloth or old quilt to cover a table or spread on the ground
- ☐ Packaged premoistened towelettes to clean hands
- ☐ Paper towels for cleanup
- ☐ Garbage bag to take care of litter
- ☐ Bug spray
- ☐ First-aid kit
- ☐ Toilet paper if you're in a remote location
- ☐ Flashlights if you'll be out after dark
- ☐ Camera

"Even when freshly washed and relieved of all obvious confections, children tend to be sticky."
—Fran Lebowitz

HAVE FUN WITH FOOD. Working on a creative concoction in the kitchen as a family can be loads of fun. Use these ideas to spur your own culinary creativity.

- ☼ Make a giant sugar cookie on a round pizza pan. Let children decorate it with icing, candies, and colored sprinkles.

- Melt 8 ounces (225 g) of chocolate in a double boiler or in the microwave, stirring occasionally until smooth. Add ½ teaspoon of peppermint extract. Pour into a heatproof serving bowl and use round butter-flavor crackers for dipping.

- Turn an ordinary cake into a clever landscape. Frost the cake, mounding extra icing to make hills. Use green-tinted coconut to make grass, and sprinkle crushed chocolate cookies to make dirt. Create a scene with small plastic toys and animals. Or, help your daughter make a princess cake. Bake a Bundt cake according to directions. Unmold it, then place a 10- to 12-inch (25- to 30-cm) doll in the center hole. Frost the cake to look like the doll's formal gown.

- Use toothpicks to roast miniature marshmallows over candlelight with a child.

- Give the children the job of creating an interesting centerpiece for the table from fresh flowers, greens, fruit, or vegetables.

- Create some new family traditions for mealtimes, such as pancakes on Saturday morning, Dad's famous chili on Sunday evenings, or homemade caramel popcorn for family movie night.

- Eat by candlelight often. Your children will love it. (Store your candles in the refrigerator; they will burn longer.)

- Plan a special family "cook day" to stockpile future meals. Make sure you have all the needed ingredients; have everyone don an apron and play your favorite music.

- Visit a farmer's market and buy fruit and vegetables to make jams, jellies, relishes, or pickles to be given as gifts to teachers during the school year.

BE A STAR. Together, compose a song, poem, or story about a special day. Videotape a family hike, carwash, or pool party for long-distance grandparents. Add a special "We miss you" message at the end.

Here are more ideas for adding (good) drama to your life.

- Put together a costume box for impromptu skits and events. Keep it handy.

- Plan a surprise "This is Your Life" celebration for someone in a low mood. Look at old photos and tell stories from the past. Tell the honoree how much his life means to you.

- Have a family awards night. Give personalized awards for silly categories such as Fastest Dish Washer, Best Lawn Mower, and Quickest to Answer Phone.
- Dress up as a family and be your own singing telegram to a family member or friend.
- Make or find a recording of a cheering crowd. Play it for a family member who's done something special, as he walks in the door.

REACH OUT. Practice hospitality and volunteer as a family in your community. This is a memorable way to teach kids the importance of giving to others. A recent survey revealed that more than a third of American households make volunteering together a part of family life.

- Brainstorm as a family about how you might serve others. You might like to do something to help older people in your neighborhood, work with a church youth program, volunteer at community sports events, or participate in an environmental program.
- Check out how your family might help serve a meal at a local homeless shelter.
- Work together as a family and host a "new kid on the block" party for a new neighbor. Make it potluck, and have old neighbors exchange names and phone numbers with the newcomers. Put together a welcome packet: include a homemade map of the immediate neighborhood; phone numbers for services and community resources; and brochures from the library, museum, and zoo.
- Select a worthy charity or mission to support as a family. Have a garage sale and donate the profits.
- Spend part of your vacation going on a mission trip as a family.

"If I were given the opportunity to present a gift to the next generation, it would be the ability for each individual to learn to laugh at himself."
—Charles Schulz

BE SILLY

- Draw funny faces on the bottom of each other's feet with washable markers. Be ready for lots of tickling and laughter.

- Spread the disease: Laughter is contagious. Start with one family member saying, "Ha." The next one says, "Ha, ha," continuing around the table, each person adding a "ha," until you lose track of who's on what "ha."

- Try this frown-remover recipe: Look at someone else or look in the mirror and frown. That takes seventy-two muscles. Now try smiling—it requires only fourteen muscles. See who can frown or smile the longest.

- Write your family's versions of Murphy's Law. Here are three to get you started.

    1. The chances of a piece of bread falling with the grape-jelly-side down is directly proportional to the cost of the carpet.

    2. Wet towels left in the back of your car mildew faster than those stuffed under the bed.

    3. The phone call you get up from dinner to answer because you think it is important will be from a telemarketer.

"The great man is he who does not lose his child's heart." —Mencius

A DOZEN WAYS TO ENJOY BIG ENTERTAINMENT—LOCALLY

Plan a day of fun with your family in your own community.

1. Explore a local museum. To make this fun for your kids, try having a museum scavenger hunt. Before you go, ask the museum for information about its exhibits. Make a list of items for the kids to search for in the museum. Ask them to write down a certain fact about what they find. After the children have located all the items, let them choose a prize from the museum souvenir shop. They'll not only have fun but learn something in the process.

2. Get up early, watch the sun rise, and cook breakfast out at a park.

3. Get rolls of quarters from the bank and take the kids to a mini amusement park to enjoy the rides and arcade games.

4. Go on a bike hike as a family. Ride to a favorite eating spot, then ride back.

5. Give each child a certain amount of money and go to garage sales or flea markets. They'll love shopping for treasures.

6. Call your local parks and recreation department and ask about available programs and activities your family might enjoy.

7. Invite other families to meet at a park for a picnic. Fly kites, throw Frisbees, or divide into teams and play softball.

8. Go on a "Where will we end up?" adventure in your car. Starting at your home, flip a coin each time you stop to see which direction you turn: heads, you turn left, and tails, you turn right. Set a time limit, and see where you land. Then take the family out for ice cream.

9. Check to see if there's a place you can pick berries or fruit close by. Go as a family, then come home and make a cobbler together.

10. Pack a picnic lunch, swimming equipment, and your camera. Spend the day at a local water park.

11. Have an old-movie marathon on a rainy day. First give each family member a certain amount of money to spend on the snacks of his choice. Go to the grocery store together. When you come home, turn off the phone and put a "Please do not disturb" sign on your front door. Then relax and enjoy the shows together.

12. Go on a family fishing expedition at a nearby lake or river.

"To improve the golden moment of opportunity, and catch the good that is within our reach, is the great art of life." —Samuel Johnson

SAVE THE MEMORIES

Always keep your camera and video camera loaded with film or digital memory and stored in the same location. There is nothing more frustrating than trying to preserve a precious moment only to discover the batteries are dead, there is no film, or, even worse, you can't find the camera.

Here are suggestions from a professional photographer on how to take great photos:

- Invest in a good camera.
- Use high-speed film so lighting is less critical.
- Shoot more face, less feet.
- Give your subjects time to relax before you press the shutter.
- Get down on kids' level to photograph them.
- Experiment with light for different effects. Noon light creates dramatic shadows; early-morning light gives a softer look.
- Capture spontaneous expressions rather than posed smiles.
- Avoid harsh shadows by photographing people away from walls.
- Make sure your background doesn't overwhelm the people you're photographing. Use a field or the sky.
- To avoid the disappointing picture in which subjects close their eyes the minute you click the shutter, make a noise just before pressing the button.
- When photographing a group, avoid a stacked look by staggering the heights in the back row.
- Shoot from different angles. Get above your subject and shoot down, or vice versa.
- Use your flash even when you don't think you need to; your subjects will appear more distinct.
- Avoid red eyes in photographs by adding light in the room: switch on lamps and pull window coverings. You can also ask your subject to glance at a bright light just before you take the photo.
- Get a picture with a soft effect by wrapping toilet tissue around your flash.
- Heavier folks will photograph better if you ask them to show their teeth when they smile, and to gently stick out their chins while standing up straight and still.
- It may seem obvious, but be sure your subject is in the center of the picture.
- Photograph dark objects in front of a light background and vice versa.
- When photographing groups, don't stand them all an equal distance from the camera. Put a few closer and a few farther away.
- Press the shutter button gently—don't jerk.
- Ask subjects to wear bright clothes.
- Keep extra film or a memory card and batteries handy.

GETTING TO KNOW YOUR NEIGHBORS IS IMPORTANT

You can work together to make your neighborhood a safer place for outdoor play, designate "safe" houses where children may go if they are being harassed and warn each other of suspicious goings-on in your area, and you can watch each other's homes, pick up each other's paper and mail when you're on vacation. Here are ways to promote friendship, networking, and safety in your neighborhood this summer.

- Create and distribute a master contact list. Interested families can provide names, addresses, phone numbers, ages of children, and family hobbies. Also, get everyone's input on favorite stores and services in your area.
- Develop a neighborhood website to post important and just-for-fun information, exchange recipes, list coming events, etc. You can do this for free via Yahoo (www.yahoo.com) and Neighborhood Link (www.neighborhoodlink.com)
- Start a monthly grill-out held at different folks' houses.
- Coordinate a neighborhood-wide garage sale or start a crime-watch program.
- Join in a common cause. Gather a group to lobby officials for a needed stop sign or to add speed bumps to your street.
- Be alert for ways to celebrate each other's occasions—big and small: tie helium balloons on a mailbox for a child's birthday, tie a big pink or blue bow on a lamppost when a new baby arrives; welcome a college student back home with his favorite pound cake.
- Pitch in and help elderly neighbors with yard work and light maintenance.
- Practice generosity by loaning yard tools. (First paint handles a bright color first so they'll remember the tools belong to you).
- Practice bartering. Find a couple of like-minded families who'd be willing to swap child care. Or barter help with big projects: "I'll help you paint your house if you'll help me paint mine."
- Host a "New Kid on the Block" party for new neighbors. Make it potluck.

LAUNCH A SUMMERTIME PLAY GROUP

Starting a summertime play group (in which moms with similar age kids take turns planning activities and supervising one another's kids as they play) is a great way to give each other a little child-free time for appointments, shopping, or relaxing by the pool (uninterrupted) with a good book. To start a play group with moms in your area, schedule a meeting to discuss the following:

1. How many children will be in the group. Four kids in the group is optimal for the under-four set, especially if there is only one parent on duty.

2. What the schedule will be. Two hours is plenty for toddlers and preschoolers to play in a group. You might allow 15 minutes to get settled, 30 minutes of a preplanned craft or activity, 15 minutes for a snack, 45 minutes of outdoor or free play, and 15 minutes of rest while listening to a book or music.

3. When the group will meet, and how often. Mornings tend to work best because young children are less tired before lunch and more willing to cooperate with other kids and try new things.

4. Where the group will meet. The host's home is typical, but you can also decide to meet at a local playground or community center.

5. How you will handle fights, separation anxiety, and other issues.

6. Special dietary or activity restrictions, or allergies. You might want to create a master list of mom-approved snack foods and activities. (Be sure to include back-up plans for rainy days.)

7. Safety precautions and how you will handle emergencies.

8. Contact information. Make sure you get each mom's address, home phone number, cell phone number, email address, and an additional emergency phone number in case she cannot be reached.

It's a good idea to put everything in writing and give each mom a copy of the guidelines before the children get together for the first time. When it's your turn to entertain all the tots, plan ahead so the supplies and snacks you'll need for hosting are easily accessible.

CHAPTER TEN

Roadmap for Stress-Free Travel

*"Let us go singing as far as we go;
the road will be less tedious."* —Virgil

*W*HAT COMES TO MIND WHEN YOU THINK about summer travel? Whining and bickering in the backseat? Expensive tourist traps? Coming home more exhausted than you were before you left?

Family vacations are fraught with potential for frustration. Smart planning can reduce stress in many areas so that everyone—Mom included—will have a good time. The ideas in this section will help you plan a summer vacation that refreshes your family, respects your checkbook, and makes positive memories for a lifetime.

START PLANNING—THE SOONER THE BETTER

- Search the Internet or write to the visitors' bureau or chamber of commerce in the state and city of your destination, as well as the ones you will pass through. Request sightseeing brochures, a map, and info about lodging, local activities, and restaurants.

- Schedule a family meeting to talk about the trip budget and each member's expectations and desires. Estimate the costs of different ideas, then prioritize the list. Make sure you honor some of your kids' wishes.

- Search for affordable lodging. Ask friends or travel agents for tips, and compare prices on the Internet. Take into consideration the numbers of beds, baths, rooms; laundry and kitchen facilities; kid-friendly activities; babysitting services; and sports amenities.

- Make sure local restaurants have kids' menus.
- Decide how many meals you'll make and how many you'll buy.
- Before you book a room, be sure to ask about all discounts.
- Read the fine print. Brochures and photos don't guarantee anything.
- Beware of travel packages that require a tour of resort property.
- Consider vacations at a national park.
- Start a reading program just for the trip. If kids meet their reading quota, they can earn a cash prize on the last day. (Reading fiction or nonfiction about the place you are visiting will build their excitement when they see the place in real life.)
- Let your kids start earning spending money. That way they can select their own souvenirs, and when they're out of money, they're done shopping.
- Plan to do postvacation laundry at a Laundromat, where you can do it all at once and sort the mail while you're waiting. And try to build in a one-day buffer between returning home from vacation and going back to work or school.

"We are not creatures of circumstance; we are creators of circumstance." —Benjamin Disraeli

BEFORE YOU LEAVE HOME

- Guarantee your room for late arrival, no matter when you plan to get there.
- Know each credit card's existing balance and credit limit.
- Put your name and address on all of your luggage, and always keep it within sight in public places.
- Plan to start driving early.
- If your accommodations include a kitchen, plan your meals and make a shopping list for when you arrive. Bring small items like spices from home. Freeze a favorite family dish ahead and transport it in a cooler.
- Highlight your route on a map so kids can track progress.
- Get the car tuned up and check the air pressure in your tires.
- Take along a book you can read aloud to the family before you go to bed at night. Choose one you can start and finish on the trip.
- Get office clothes dry-cleaned while you're away.
- Leave a meal in the freezer at home so you'll have dinner almost ready when you get back.

DON'T SPEND MONEY YOU DON'T HAVE TO

- Drink water with meals.
- Use your cell phone (depending on your plan) or the pay phone in the hotel lobby rather than the phone in your room.
- Bring your own snacks. Avoid the in-room refrigerator.
- Skip room service.
- Don't wait until you're running on fumes to buy gas, so you can look for competitive prices. Check oil and tires occasionally.

"Travel . . . is a part of education."
—*Francis Bacon*

CREATE KID-FRIENDLY TRAVEL. To make sure the kids have a great time, keep them in mind as you put together a summer travel plan. Here are some tips.

- Plan and do less than you think you can during the trip so that no one comes home exhausted.
- Get recommendations from other families on the best places to go.
- Schedule alone-time for family members who need it.
- Don't expect kids to like the same things Mom and Dad do. Plan around the kids.
- Try something different: a bicycle tour, a family cruise, working at a guest ranch.
- Make family—not the office—your focus.
- Have your kids start a trip scrapbook, collecting things each day to put in it, such as postcards, a leaf, a to-go menu. Record humorous incidents and special memories. The writer in the family could write a travel narrative.
- Make trip videos as you go, and watch them at night in your hotel. An older child could be in charge of making the video. Or rent videos from a local store rather than from the hotel.
- Take advantage of local free entertainment: tours, museums, concerts.

PACK SMART. Here are some ideas for traveling lightly but efficiently:

- If possible, take only clothes made of lighter, hand-washable fabrics.
- Pack socks and belts inside shoes.
- Don't forget emergency items such as medication for sunburn and stomach upset, and Band-Aids.
- Pack last what you'll need first, such as pajamas.
- Pack wrinkle-resistant clothing.
- Zip nylons into a resealable plastic bag to avoid snags.
- Have each family member make a list of what he's taking. He can check off each item as he repacks it for going home. This list will also serve as an inventory of what's in each bag for insurance claim purposes or in case luggage goes AWOL.
- Take smaller versions of big-bottle products like shampoo.
- Button buttons, zip zippers, and close snaps on clothes before packing. They'll retain their shape better.
- Squeeze excess air from bottles and tubes before sealing. You'll have fewer leaks.
- Assemble kids' clothes by complete day's outfit, and put each in a plastic bag. Choosing an outfit every day will be simple!
- Take along a small amount of laundry detergent for hand-washing, and some clothespins. You can use these on hangers to dry clothes.
- Take along a large plastic dirty-clothes bag and pack a collapsible bag for the souvenirs you buy.
- Take an electrical converter, if necessary.
- Leave a copy of your itinerary, the numbers on your traveler's checks, credit cards you won't need, and copies of your passports/visas at home.

REDUCE HUNDREDS OF DETAILS TO A DOABLE LIST. You've got countless details and items to remember to pack before a trip, no matter what the ages of your kids or where you're headed. Use these lists to help you remember every little thing-and some you hadn't thought to take along.

For any summer trip:	
Wallet/cash	Sunglasses
Credit cards and/or traveler's checks	Watch
Eyeglasses/contacts	Medical insurance cards
	Prescription and other medications

Itineraries, tickets, and reservation-confirmation numbers

Maps and directions

Tote bag or backpack for day use

Camera, film, batteries, charger and memory card for digital camera

Toys, playing cards, small games

Flashlight and batteries

Umbrellas, rain ponchos, or jackets

Large plastic bags for laundry and wet items

Small plastic bags

Disposable wipes

Travel alarm

Sewing kit

First-aid kit

Snacks/gum

Water/juice, no-spill cups

Paper towels, tissues

Cell phone programmed with emergency numbers, charger

Maps/road atlas

Toothbrushes, toothpaste, dental floss, and mouthwash

Deodorant

Combs, brushes, hair accessories, blow-dryer (check hotel online to see if it provides a blow-dryer)

Shampoo, conditioner

Sunscreen and lip balm

Lotion

Insect repellent

Sunburn and rash salves

Shaving items

Makeup

Nail clippers, scissors, and emery board

Tweezers

Cotton balls and swabs

Feminine hygiene products

Sneakers or walking shoes

Outfits for each day

Underwear

Sleepwear

Swimwear

Hiking gear

Accessories

Outerwear

Pillows

Address book and stamps

Extra duffel or tote bag for souvenirs

Stain-removal stick

For baby:

Car seat

Diaper bag

Disposable diapers

Changing pad

Baby powder and lotion

Resealable plastic bags

Wet wipes

Nursing pads/burp pads

Bibs

Baby food and spoon

Bottles, nipples, and caps

Formula and/or juice

Pacifiers

Changes of clothing

Jacket or sweater

Collapsible stroller with canopy
or umbrella

Front or back child-carrying pack
or sling-style child carrier

Portable crib/playpen

Blankets

Waterproof sheets

Bathing supplies

Large plastic bags for wet clothes

Lotion for diaper rash

Teething medicine

Nasal aspirator

For a trip to a theme park:

Sunscreen, lip balm

Insect repellent

Hats or visors

Plastic canteens or water bottles with
shoulder straps (fill with ice from
hotel at start of day)

Camera and film or memory card

Small blank book and pen or plain
white T-shirt and fabric marker for
character autographs

Lightweight rain poncho

Moleskin (in case of blisters)

Fanny pack or small backpack

Travel first-aid supplies:

Adult aspirin, acetaminophen,
or ibuprofen

Baby aspirin, acetaminophen,
or substitute

Dramamine

Antibacterial gel for hand washing
without water

Antiseptic ointment

Insect repellent

Ipecac

Sunscreen

Ointment for insect bites and sunburn

Adhesive bandages in various sizes,
adhesive tape, and gauze pads

Triple-antibiotic cream for
small wounds

Premoistened towelettes

Tissues

Antihistamine or allergy medication

Antidiarrheal and constipation
medicine

Antacids

Cough medicine and/or throat lozenges

Petroleum jelly

Oral and rectal thermometers

Tweezers and needle (for removing
splinters)

Fingernail scissors

Cotton balls and or swabs

Antiseptic soap

Moleskin in case of blisters

First-aid book

MAKE SURE THE SUMMER SKIES ARE FRIENDLY. Trouble-proof your trip via aircraft by using these tips.

- Join frequent-flier programs. Some offer advance boarding privileges.
- Avoid booking the last flight of the day. If it's canceled for some reason, you're stranded overnight.
- When traveling abroad, photocopy the information page of your passport. Carry a copy separately when you travel.
- Take a just-in-case carry-on bag of daily medications, a sewing kit, contact lens products, and so on. Consider adding a change of clothes.
- Look for discount tickets, but read the fine print.
- Ask airlines or travel agents about discounts for families flying together.
- Ask if land-air packages are available for your destination.
- Try to make connections in a hub city rather than taking a more expensive nonstop flight.
- Take several individually wrapped small toys to help the trip pass quickly for small children.
- Try to take flights that have movies—kids love this.
- Bring along bottles of water and snacks in case you're thirsty or hungry before meals are served.
- Try to arrive at the airport closest to your final destination.
- Reserve bulkhead or emergency-exit seats for more legroom.
- Order kid-friendly meals at least twenty-four hours before departure time.
- Take some gum along for help unblocking ears during takeoff and landing.
- If traveling with a baby, be prepared for delays by taking along extra formula, diapers, and other supplies.
- Wear loose, comfortable clothing and shoes. Make sure kids' clothes are easy to fasten and unfasten during restroom visits.
- Have each child bring a backpack of small toys and games.
- Tie a bright ribbon around handles of carry-on bags to make them easily identifiable.
- Don't fly within twelve hours of having dental work.
- Ask for a pillow and blanket as soon as you're seated.

SWERVING AROUND CAR-RENTAL CASH TRAPS

- Check to see if your auto-insurance policy covers rental cars. Buying insurance when renting a car is always expensive and often not necessary. Some credit cards offer automatic coverage when you charge a car rental.

- The convenience of dropping a car off at a site other than where you rented it usually comes at a cost—fifteen to thirty dollars. Shop around and know the costs before taking this option.

- For the best rental-car rates, book advertised specials as soon as you see them; rental companies change their rates quickly. Consider using smaller rental companies with off-site lots. Many charge up to 20 percent less than the bigger companies do.

- Plan flight arrivals and departures for the same time of day to avoid being charged an extra day's rate for just a couple of hours' use of a car.

- Look into taking a shuttle or public transportation to your lodging destination, then rent a car the next day—saving one day's rental cost.

- Many rental companies add as much as three dollars a day or ten dollars a rental for each additional driver. Shop around for competitive rates. Don't try to save money by not adding additional drivers to the contract. If you have an accident, the company may withhold insurance benefits. This can cost you big money.

- Always inspect a rental car before driving. Report anything missing or broken immediately. Make sure the damage is noted on your contract so you won't get charged.

- Remember, all fifty states require child safety seats. Bring your own car seat from home. Or, when reserving your car, tell the agent you'll need a child safety seat, too. They are available for a nominal daily or weekly rate.

17 WAYS TO AVOID SAYING "DON'T MAKE ME STOP THIS CAR!"

By planning ahead, you can save yourself from the bickering in the backseat—and the front.

1. Don't wait until the last minute to get ready. Share the many errands required before a trip: servicing the car, filling up with gas, installing the proper safety seats, and packing the night before you leave. Go to bed early if possible.

2. Let your child pack a travel box with small toys, art supplies, and other treasures. Add a couple of new toys for surprise treats. A 13 x 9 x 2-inch (32.5 x 22.5 x 5-cm) plastic bin with a lid doubles as a storage box and lap desk in the car.

3. Pack your sense of humor and a positive attitude. This will help you survive bad weather, rude people, poor service, and a host of other surprises and inconveniences.

4. Wear loose, comfortable clothing and shoes. Make sure kids' clothes are easy to get into and out of during restroom visits. Have a tote bag or small plastic crate in the car specifically for kids to put their socks and shoes in when they take them off.

5. Relieve last-minute stress by glancing at the Summer Vacation Exit Checklist before you leave the house. (See page 99.)

6. Bring along music and books on cassette or CD the whole family will enjoy. Also bring joke and brainteaser books. They come in handy if you have to wait to get your car repaired. They're also fun to read together while waiting for food to be served in a restaurant. It's also a good idea to rent a mobile video/DVD unit and bring along some kid-friendly videos/DVDs to help the time pass in the car.

7. Cut out the portion of a map with the highways you'll be traveling, then highlight the route with a yellow marker. Glue your map to a piece of cardboard and laminate it with clear Con-Tact paper. Kids will enjoy tracking your progress.

8. Take along Colorforms for young children. They work great on windows.

9. Play "Look for the License Plates." Make a photocopy of a United States map. Glue the map to a piece of cardboard and cover it with clear Con-Tact paper. Every time you spot a license plate from a different state, color in the state with a washable marker. When you arrive at your destination, count the number of states you marked. Wipe off the board and play the game again on the way home.

10. Have the driver and the referee share responsibilities. If possible, let each parent be relieved of his or her duties at regular intervals. Interstate traffic may be a delightful change for one parent, whereas the other might have a fresh supply of patience for the backseat. When both parents are tired or a backseat catastrophe occurs, it might be a good time to stop for a snack, air out the car, change the seating arrangement, then resume the trip by playing a great CD or DVD you've been saving for an hour of desperation.

11. Require a five- to ten-minute period of silence each hour. (This can be a real sanity saver.)

12. Stop every two hours. Let each person have a turn deciding when to stop. For example, an eight-year-old might dictate that at 2:17 you'll stop for ice cream. When that time comes, go to the first place that offers ice cream. Dad might determine that at 3:54 he wants to stop at the first bait store you see after that time.

13. Carry a small notebook to keep pertinent trip information. For future reference, take notes along the way about the places you enjoyed or that gave you good service, such as gas stations, motels, and restaurants. Make note of negative experiences, too, so you won't make the same mistake twice.

14. Diversity helps keep kids content—let them exchange toys, snacks, and seats during the trip.

15. Offer kids water while traveling rather than pop or juice. They like water less, so they'll drink less, and you'll visit restrooms less!

16. Stop at points of interest along the way to your final destination (including "silly" ones your kids would get a kick out of). This makes the trip pass more quickly.

17. Relax. Remember, the object is to have fun, not cover a record number of miles each day or visit an unrealistic number of visitor centers.

"Have a heart that never hardens, and a temper that never fires, and a touch that never hurts."
—*Charles Dickens*

SUMMER VACATION EXIT CHECKLIST. Don't panic. You locked the door, shut off the coffeepot, and closed the garage. All because you used this list!

- ☐ Check to make sure you have all tickets and that everyone over age 15 has a photo ID.
- ☐ Make sure all bags and gear are in the car.
- ☐ Put some wipes in the glove compartment or carry-on bag.
- ☐ Secure items you couldn't pack until the last moment (child's security blanket, favorite stuffed animal, pillows, toiletry items).
- ☐ Confirm that you've stopped newspaper and mail or have arranged for a neighbor to pick them up.
- ☐ Confirm arrangements for plant and pet care.
- ☐ Fill prescriptions to cover your time away.
- ☐ Pick up any spare keys you've hidden outside.
- ☐ Give your itinerary and phone numbers to a friend, relative, or neighbor so you can be reached in case of emergency. (It's also a good idea to leave a key with someone so he or she can check on your house while you're away.)
- ☐ Unplug coffeemaker, small appliances, TV, electronic equipment, and computers to protect them from power surges while you're gone.
- ☐ Check to see if the stove and oven are turned off.
- ☐ Remove milk and other perishables from the refrigerator.
- ☐ Make sure refrigerator and freezer doors are securely shut.
- ☐ Wash dirty dishes and run disposal.
- ☐ Take out all garbage.
- ☐ Turn off water supply to washing machine and ice maker.
- ☐ Activate answering machine.
- ☐ Set thermostat and adjust water heater for vacation setting.
- ☐ Set automatic light timers and sprinkler system.
- ☐ Check to see that all windows and doors are secure.
- ☐ Make sure no valuables are visible from the windows.
- ☐ Arm security system.
- ☐ Exit and lock the door as well as the garage door and any outside buildings.

Safety Essentials Your Children Should Know

Before taking your kids to water parks, theme parks, or public events, take the
following precautions.

- Teach young children to recite their names, address, and phone number.
  If basic memorization is difficult for them, try singing the information to a
  familiar tune. Learn the new song together.
- Show kids how, if they get lost or need help, to dial 911 from a pay phone.
  Explain that they don't need change to use this number at a public phone.
- Tell them never to go into a public bathroom alone.
- Have your children practice being loud if they feel threatened by a stranger.
- Help your children understand that they should never leave a public place with a stranger, no matter what he says.
- Practice how to ask a policeman or other uniformed personnel for help if they need it.
- Teach your children what body parts are not okay for others to touch and train them to shout "Stop!" or "No!" if someone touches them in an off-limits place.

TWO-FAMILY SUMMER VACATIONS: MORE FUN, LESS MONEY

This summer, why not try vacationing with another family? Let these ideas simplify the planning.

1. Find a family who wants to vacation in the same place you do, and plan a meeting to discuss the details: your vacation budget, possible lodging options and prices, and available activities in the area. Be truthful on the front end about your family's likes and dislikes and budget limitations.

2. Choose accommodations big enough for both families. Ask the rental agent about the square footage and the number of bathrooms and bedrooms of

the houses or condominiums you're considering. Ask for a floor plan if it's available—then you can decide who will sleep where before you arrive. Make sure the kitchen is stocked with enough dishes for both families.

3. Agree to divide the rental cost, and appoint one person to take care of administrative details such as filling out rental papers, sending in a deposit, or confirming your stay by credit card.

4. Talk about which outings and activities you want to do together and which you want to do alone. Above all, remember that things change, so be ready to be flexible. Everyone will enjoy the trip more.

5. Decide who will be in charge of cooking which meals and divide cleanup responsibilities.

6. Make a list of supplies you'll need and divide the list. You'll save precious luggage space.

7. Be sure to pack board games, cards, and a big jigsaw puzzle for rainy-day or nightly entertainment.

8. Decide on a meeting place for the day of your departure. If you travel caravan-style, the kids can take turns riding in different cars and trading card games and CDs, which makes the trip less monotonous for them. And if one family has car trouble, the other is there to help out.

9. If you'll be traveling all day, let each family pack one picnic meal for both families. This way you don't have to bring so many items, and you cut costs by eating less in restaurants.

10. When you arrive at your vacation spot, unpack and talk to the kids about any house rules you mutually decide upon. Make sure they understand that the family room and kitchen are community territory, but each family needs privacy in their bedrooms and baths.

11. Let the parents take a turn at entertaining all the kids for one day or night of the trip. This way, each set of parents gets a break.

12. Because even the best of friends sometimes see too much of each other on a trip, plan at least two or three half-day sojourns that are single-family only.

 "All is well that ends well." —John Heywood

Trip Planner

ESTIMATED TRAVEL TIME: _____	
ENTERTAINMENT IDEAS	**TRAVEL SCHEDULE**

ENTERTAINMENT IDEAS

Books_____
_____
_____
_____
_____

Games_____
_____
_____
_____
_____

Tapes/CDs_____
_____
_____
_____
_____

DVDs_____
_____
_____
_____
_____

Travel Box and Supplies_____
_____
_____
_____
_____

Sightseeing_____
_____
_____
_____
_____
_____
_____

TRAVEL SCHEDULE

Include meals, sightseeing, overnight stops
_____
_____
_____
_____
_____
_____
_____
_____
_____
_____
_____
_____
_____
_____
_____
_____
_____
_____
_____
_____

Picnic Meals and Snacks _____
_____
_____
_____
_____
_____
_____
_____
_____
_____
_____

Important Summer Events and Occasions

EVENT	DATE
Last Day of School	
Summer Camp	
Lessons/Classes	
Vacation Bible School	
Family Vacation	
School Starts	

CHAPTER 11

Building Strong Character

"Good character, like good soup, is made at home."

—B. C. Forbes

TAKING CARE OF OUR CHILDREN'S PHYSICAL NEEDS is important, but helping them grow spiritually and develop strong character is at least as vital. It is our job as parents to shape our children's values as they grow, to give them a sense of right and wrong, and to provide them with an inner compass that will guide them through life. None of us will ever be perfect parents, nor will we raise perfect children. But one thing's for sure: if we don't teach them our values, other people will teach them theirs.

Summer is the perfect time to fan the fire of your child's faith and help him grow stronger in character. Every day you have natural opportunities to instill spiritual truth and principles for wise living in your children. But what's even more important than seizing teachable moments is setting a good example. The old adage is true: more is caught than taught. Kids won't buy a double standard. If you tell your children to live one way but you behave in another way, the message they will get is that you don't really believe what you're telling them is important.

52 WAYS TO TEACH AND LIVE THE VALUES YOU WANT YOUR CHILDREN TO EMBRACE.

   1. Be intentional. Set aside some time, either with your spouse or alone, to make a list of the values and character qualities you want to pass on to your children.

Here are some you might consider. Add your own to the list.

Honesty

Kindness

Love

Faith

Patience

Self-discipline

Commitment to community service

Loyalty

Leadership

Enthusiasm

Love of learning

A strong work ethic

Courage

Allegiance to country

Care for others

Helpfulness

Compassion

Respect

2. As you think about what you want your children to know and how you want them to grow this summer, take some time to become comfortable with your own faith. All of us need a way to answer the deep questions of life: Where did I come from? Why am I here? Where am I going? Does life have any meaning or purpose? It is only when we know the living God ourselves that we can introduce him to our children. Take a close look at who you think God is. Where did you get this information? Do you think you know the real thing, or have you constructed a mental image on your own?

3. Talk about other religions with your children and compare them with your own. Create an atmosphere in which your kids can openly ask questions and work through their beliefs. Honest wonderings, and even honest doubts, deserve straightforward discussion and answers.

4. Buy a children's version of the Bible for your child. Encourage him and reward him for reading a portion every day. Read Bible storybooks to young children who cannot read.

5. Help your child get involved in a church or synagogue youth group or Bible

study. Peers with like values can encourage each other to live up to high standards. Volunteer to have the youth group or Bible study meet at your home. Ask if you can chaperone events and trips.

6. Use your imagination to think of rewarding and stimulating ways to encourage spiritual growth in your children. Use colorful charts on poster board to record points and motivate progress. Our kids loved this one:

   - Give yourself 100 points for reading Ruth, Jonah, Esther, or Psalm 119.
   - Give yourself 250 points for reading 1 Samuel, 2 Samuel, Daniel, Mark, John, or Revelation.
   - Give yourself 450 points for reading Genesis or Exodus.

   Offer prizes for reaching designated point goals. For example, if they earn 800 points, you'll take them and a friend out to lunch at a favorite restaurant. For 700 points, they can buy a new CD. For 550 points, they can be excused from doing chores for a day. For 350 points, they earn a small treat of their choice.

7. Set up a fun and creative reward system like the one I just described to help your child memorize Scripture verses and wisdom literature. If children grow to love wisdom, they are more apt to find it sustains them through the trials everyone encounters in life.

8. Think of topics you would like your children to study, such as anger, friends, honesty, love, self-discipline, and work. Use the sample study on **Friends** for elementary-age children as a guide for making up your own. (See page 114.)

9. One night as a family, write down everything for which you are thankful.

10. When you attend a wedding, talk to your child about what being married means: the rings, the vows, the religious ceremony.

11. Pray for your children. This is the most powerful thing you can do for them. Keep a journal of your prayers.

12. Have your children fill out the **Kids' Questionnaire** (see page 113). Be ready to listen to what your kids say.

13. Remember that what you leave in your children is far more important than what you leave to them.

14. If you are the only person in your family committed to teaching your kids strong values, remember the words of Helen Keller and don't give up: "I am only one; but still I am one. I cannot do everything, but still I can do something; I will not refuse to do the something I can do."

15. When you get discouraged, keep in mind the words of Mother Teresa: "God has not called me to be successful; he has called me to be faithful." Strive to be

the best parent you can be, and do all you can to teach your kids strong values. But remember that you cannot control how your children turn out.

16. Keep a picture of your children on your desk at work or at home to remind yourself to pray for them during the day.

> "What families have in common the world around is that they are the place where people learn who they are and how to be that way."
> —Jean Illsley Clarke

17. Ask your children to pray for you, that God will help you be a good parent to them.

18. Bring back family dinnertime. Eating together is an unparalleled opportunity for family discussion of issues both large and small, and the passing on of values. Encourage conversation by not allowing TV and phone calls during dinner.

19. Talk casually and consistently with your children. When you run an errand in your car, take a child with you. Sometimes staring through a windshield is a nonthreatening time to talk about important issues.

20. Take advantage of changing seasons to remind children about God's good earth. Go fishing, camping, fruit-picking this summer. On a star-filled evening, lie on a quilt in your backyard and look at the heavens God created. Visit a farmers' market or roadside stand and delight in the various fruits and vegetables God made. Go for a walk in the woods. Talk about the many miracles of nature that we take for granted: the variety of colors and shapes, how God cares for his creatures, how all things hold together, the miracle of growth.

21. When you're swimming, running, or riding bikes together, comment about how good it is that God gave us muscles to enjoy these sports. Thank him spontaneously.

22. Send your kids to a good summer camp that embraces the values you hold. It's good for kids to hear someone else besides Mom and Dad talking about what's right and wrong.

23. Point out the small ways God is at work in your life. A miracle is not always spectacular. It might be a miracle that you get through a three-hour car trip

without sibling arguments. It might be a miracle that you finish a project on time or that there's money in the bank to pay the electric bill.

24. Sit near the front of your place of worship so your children can see what's happening and feel more involved in the worship service.

25. Sing hymns or songs from your faith as you put your child to bed at night.

26. Ask yourself this question about your young child's behavior: What disrespectful behavior am I laughing at today that I do not want to see repeated and exaggerated when my child gets older?

27. Create a warm and welcoming atmosphere in your home so your kids and their friends will want to hang out there. They'll have a safe, fun place to go, and you'll know what they're doing. Keep plenty of soda and snacks on hand, and be willing to put up with some mess and some louder-than-pleasant music if they're older.

28. Take a look at yourself from your children's perspective. Do they look up to you as the type of adult they want to be someday?

29. Don't bury your head in the sand. Listen to your children's music. Especially find out what they're listening to via headphones. Question the lyrics. When I had teenagers, I enrolled in an exercise class that played popular music, not only for the exercise, but to keep up with what my kids were hearing on the radio. Ask your kids if they understand the lyrics of their favorite songs. Research shows that when our minds receive an image six times, it becomes indelibly etched there. Don't foolishly think that lyrics with messages about casual sex, rebellion, and suicide are not affecting your child's decisions.

30. Help your kids network with other kids who have like values and ambitions. Before our boys started high school, we hosted a party during the summer for kids they had met from other schools who would soon be attending the same high school.

31. Be vigilant about your children's friends. If they ask to spend time with someone whose values and habits are questionable, let them have the friend over to your house. If you see that the relationship would not be a healthy one for your child and that your child may not be strong enough be the leader, talk about this openly.

32. When they behave poorly, make sure they understand what they did was wrong, why it was wrong, and what they need to do to make amends and change their behavior.

33. "Do not let any unwholesome talk come out of your mouths, but only what is helpful for building others up according to their needs, that it may benefit those who listen" (Ephesians 4:29 NIV). Talk about the meaning of this verse

as a family. Sit down together and make a list of the names and negative phrases you would like to eliminate from your family's vocabulary: dummy, stupid, punk, I don't like you, you make me sick. Talk about how each person feels when these things are said to him or her. Rid them from your conversation. Put each person in charge of him- or herself. Have a chart with each person's name. Put a check mark by the name of the person who has a slip of the tongue and uses one of the off-limits words or phrases.

34. Teach your children the importance of valuing the personal property of others. Have a house rule that family members—Mom and Dad included—are to ask before borrowing something that belongs to someone else.

35. Create your own set of family rules concerning acceptable behavior. Set a goal for every family member to strive to live by them—Mom and Dad too. For example, a child's rule might be, "I will not leave my wet bathing suit on the floor." One of Mom's rules might be, "I will try not to go ballistic when you leave a wet bathing suit on the bathroom floor."

36. Identify the consistent conflicts in your home that cause tempers to flair: whose turn it is to feed the dog or do the dishes, how many minutes someone gets to play a video game, how much time may be spent on the telephone. Meet together as a family and map out simple guidelines of fairness. Post them in a conspicuous location.

37. Volunteer as a family in your community. The most popular activities include helping older people, working with youth or religious programs, assisting in sports or school programs, and serving the homeless. You could also do something as simple as saving aluminum cans, redeeming them at a recycling center, and donating the profits. Or, you could volunteer to help paint or weed and mow the lawn of a nonprofit organization's building. This is a memorable way to teach kids the importance of giving to others.

38. Teach courage. Make sure your children know that they must stand for something, or they'll fall for anything.

39. Walk out of movies that offend your values, and instruct your kids to do the same. Many theaters will give you a refund or rain check if you ask.

 What we leave in our children is more important than what we leave to them.

40. Keep the flame alive. Make your marriage an ongoing priority. It's one of the greatest things you can do for your children.

41. Express your hopes for your children. Talk about your dreams for them-that they will live by strong values.

42. Discuss compromise. Make sure your kids know that if they have to do the wrong thing to stay on the team, they are on the wrong team. Talk about the meaning of this adage: "You're not necessarily on the right track just because it's a well-beaten path."

43. Build a movie library. Start a collection of DVDs or videos that entertain your kids and teach them strong values at the same time.

44. Teach respect for authority. Do not allow your children to behave, in word or action, disrespectfully to you or other adults. Daily events offer many occasions for this, but children need to learn it from your example. Do you disregard the law or bad-mouth the school authorities? Remember, your children are always learning.

45. Honor heroic behavior. Point out instances in the news and everyday life in which people have been heroic.

46. Remind your children that their beliefs about God may be questioned and even ridiculed. Make sure they are grounded in what is true and are ready to defend their faith.

47. Supervise your kids' intake. Monitor Internet time and television watching. Be alert for programs that promote values different from the ones you want your children to learn.

48. Be aware that viewing violence on TV increases aggressiveness, instills fear of becoming a victim, promotes indifference to victims of violence, and stimulates appetite for more violence. Decide how much you will allow your children to watch TV each day, and stick to your decision. Decide what they can watch as well. Make sure they turn on the TV to see a specific show, not to just see what's on.

49. To use television in a positive way, when your child really wants to see a show, watch it with him or her. Then discuss the positives and negatives that he or she learned from the program. Here are some questions to guide your discussion:

   • How would you rate this show on a scale from one to ten?

   • What was the program's message?

   • Could you identify with any of the characters?

   • What would you do to help any of the characters?

   • Was there anything in the program you did not agree with?

- Did you feel this show portrayed life as it really is?
- Was this program worth your time?
- What in the program uplifted you or motivated you to be a better person?

50. As you drive down the street or walk the mall, talk to your children about the value of each human being and the dignity of his or her job. Teach your kids to appreciate the contribution of the mail carrier, the auto repair person, the utility worker, the doctor, the banker, the grocery store employee. Talk about the skills and preparation necessary for each job.

51. Children are bombarded daily with the message that their value depends on physical attractiveness, drinking the right soft drink, and wearing the right brand of clothes. Remind them daily of their value and uniqueness as a person, and your unconditional love.

52. Start a collection of good books that teach strong character qualities and values to your children.

Kids' Questionnaire

We would like to have your honest answers to these questions. Please tell us how you really feel, nor what you think we want to hear.

How important do you feel? Write a "+" if you feel more important than what is listed; "−" if you feel less important; and "=" if you feel as important as what is listed.

To my dad, I feel more or less important than...

_____ his work

_____ his tools

_____ his friends

_____ his rest, recreation

_____ his car

_____ his relationship with Mom

_____ his relationship with God

_____ his yard

_____ the church

_____ outside activities or meetings

_____ _____

_____ _____

I would feel more important to my dad if...

_____

_____

I would feel more important to my dad if he would...

_____

_____

To my mom, I feel more or less important than...

_____ her work

_____ her house

_____ her friends

_____ her rest, recreation

_____ her clothes

_____ her relationship with Dad

_____ her relationship with God

_____ her kitchen

_____ the church

_____ outside activities or meetings

_____ _____

_____ _____

I would feel more important to my mom if...

_____

_____

I would feel more important to my mom if she would...

_____

_____

I feel really proud of myself when I _____

_____

I am really good at _____

_____

I really enjoy _____

_____

I feel worthless when I _____

_____

If I could change one thing about myself, it would be_____

_____

_____

Friends

Look up the following verses and write down what friends do for each other.

Proverbs 17:7 _____

_____

Proverbs 27:6 _____

_____

Ecclesiastes 4:10 _____

_____

What special things can you do for your friends?

_____

_____

What does God say about the wrong kinds of friends in these verses?

Proverbs 22:24 _____

_____

Proverbs 1:10 _____

_____

Proverbs 16:28 _____

_____

Proverbs 16:29 _____

_____

Read 1 Samuel 18:1-4. How was Jonathan a good friend to David?

_____

_____

If you would like to schedule a Summer Survival seminar in your area, you can e-mail Kathy at familymanager@familymanager.com. Visit www.familymanager.com for more resources and helpful advice on how to raise great kids and be a successful family manager.

Safety Check

"Better safe than sorry"

—Proverb

Summertime means that your kids will be spending more time outdoors. It's important to prepare your yard and outside areas for maximum safety and enjoyment. Before school lets out, carve out some time to perform an outdoor safety check and tackle any tasks that will help make your yard a safe haven for play.

- Check wooden decks for splinters
- Install a latch on the door leading to your balcony or yard.
- Regularly check swings and other play equipment for rust, loose screws, splintering wood, or sharp edges.
- Make sure children's play equipment is securely anchored before use. Test it yourself to detect potentially unsafe structures.
- Put covers on swing chains to avoid caught fingers and torn clothes.
- Put wood chips, sand, or mulch under your swing set or play area. The deeper the fill goes, the safer your child will be in case of a fall. Make sure the fill extends out far enough that if a child is propelled from a swing, he will still land on a softer surface.
- If your yard is not fenced off from the street, establish a safety zone along the front yard that ids know to stay inside. Consider buying orange safety cones (available at athletic supply stores) and teach children not to go past them.

- Keep the play area clean of pet droppings. Keep cats out of the sandbox by covering it when not in use.

- Make sure wooden fences have rounded, well-sanded posts and chain-link fences have no barbs sticking up.

- Get rid of highly poisonous or toxic plants growing in your back or front yard. Call your local poison-control center for a list of dangerous plants in your area.

- Teach kids to identify and steer clear of poison ivy. If you find it in your yard, dig it up carefully and don't let your children touch you until you've showered with plenty of soap and put on clean clothes. Wash the clothes and sneakers you were wearing and clean any tools that touched the ivy, as the oil will stay on the garments and tools.

- After a rainy period, remove any mushrooms or toadstools since they could be poisonous.

- If you spot wasp nests, wait till after dark to spray them with insecticide. Wasps cling to their nest after sunset and will not attack you.

- Make sure toxic chemicals, solvents, paints, and gasoline are inaccessible to children in your garage.

- Store ladders out of reach, or secure them to the wall horizontally, so they will not tempt kids to climb.

- Keep your car locked to prevent your child from climbing inside, activating the garage door opener, or knocking the car out of gear.

BE PREPARED

It's important to be prepared to deal with those inevitable injuries-from minor knee scrapes to life-threatening wounds-that can happen when children are playing. A well-stocked first-aid kit and basic over-the-counter medications are key to emergency preparedness. Below are items to keep on hand, plus you should ask your pediatrician for recommendations pertaining to your children's specific health issues. Always store all medications out of the reach of small children but easily accessible to adults and baby-sitters.

- Activated charcoal (use only if instructed by Poison Control Center)
- Antibiotic ointment
- Antiseptic wipes
- Adhesive bandage strips (various sizes and waterproof)
- Aloe vera gel

- Antibacterial hand wash
- Antihistamine cream or gel
- Calamine lotion
- Disposable medical exam gloves (latex or vinyl)
- Gauze pads and roller gauze (assorted sizes)
- Hydrocortisone cream or ointment
- Non-aspirin pain relievers for children
- Saline solution
- Scissors
- Self-adhering roller bandage
- Syrup of Ipecac (use only if instructed by Poison Control Center)
- Thermometer
- Tweezers

DIY Ice Packs

Store small and large ice packs in your freezer to have on hand for treating bumps and bruises. To make your own ice pack, mix 1 cup rubbing alcohol with 2 cups of water in a 1 quart-size, self-sealing plastic freezer bag. For a large ice pack, mix 2 cups of rubbing alcohol with 4 cups of water in a 1 gallon-size, self-sealing plastic freezer bag. The alcohol-water mixture will only freeze to a slushy state. After using, return it to the freezer for next time.

Tick Bite Essentials

If you live in a wooded area or go camping in tick territory and begin to experience flu-like symptoms within a week to 10 days following your campout, you may have a tick-bite reaction. Almost all tick diseases can be treated effectively with antibiotics if caught early enough. If you have any of the following symptoms, call your doctor immediately.

- Rash
- A bruise-like circular area surrounding the area of a bite.
- Recurring fever, chills,
- Severe headaches
- Muscle pain, stiffness
- Neck pain
- Swollen joints
- Partial paralysis
- Facial paralysis
- Nausea and vomiting

Make Your Own Tick Removal Kit

In a cosmetic purse pack fine-point tweezers, packs of alcohol swabs, needle and a pack of matches.

IMPORTANT FORMS AND INFORMATION

Make copies of the following forms and keep them in a file. Use as needed when babysitters, grandparents or other people are caring for your children while you're away.

Emergency Contact Information

Home # _____ Office # _____ Cell phone # _____

Home Address_____Zip _____

Directions from nearest major intersection _____

_____

_____

_____

Ambulance # _____ Pet emergency # _____

Poison control # _____ Alarm company # _____

Location - Syrup of Ipecac _____ First aid kit _____

Physician: Name _____ Phone _____

Hospital: Name _____ Phone _____

Other Contacts

Relative _____ Relationship _____

Address _____

Home # _____ Office # _____ Cell phone # _____

Relative _____ Relationship _____

Address _____

Home # _____ Office # _____ Cell phone # _____

Neighbor _____

Address _____

Home # _____ Office # _____ Cell phone # _____

Friend _____ Relationship _____

Address _____

Home # _____ Office # _____ Cell phone # _____

General Information for Babysitters

Security system instructions _____

_____

Location of . . .

    Flashlights _____

    Fire extinguishers _____

    Fuse or breaker box_____

    Water shutoff_____

    Syrup of Ipecac _____

Fire escape plan _____

_____

Food/Beverages/Snacks _____

_____

Meal Instructions_____

_____

Medications _____

    Dosage/Times/Instructions _____

_____

Other _____

_____

House Rules

    Bedtime _____

    Homework_____

    TV/Computer_____

    Friends _____

Emergency Identification Information

Distribute copies of this form to friends, family, and authorities in an emergency.

Full name _____

Name called _____

Address_____

Phone_____ Social security number _____

Date of birth_____ Place of birth _____

Sex _____ Blood type _____ Ethnic background _____

Height _____ Weight _____ Eyes _____ Hair _____

Identifying features _____

_____

Date of attached photograph _____

Emergency contacts

Name _____ Relationship _____

Address _____ Phone _____

Name _____ Relationship _____

Address _____ Phone _____

Name _____ Relationship _____

Address _____ Phone _____

Name _____ Relationship _____

Address _____ Phone _____

Physician _____ Phone _____

Dentist _____ Phone _____

Local police/Missing persons phone _____

Have local police fingerprint your family/children and attach.

The National Center for Missing & Exploited Children 1-800-THE-LOST

Consent for Emergency Medical Treatment of a Minor*

Child's Name_____ Date of birth _____/_____/_____

Social Security Number _____

Address_____

_____

Child's regular physician_____Phone _____

Address_____

_____

Health insurance company _____Phone _____

Name of primary insured _____

Social security number of primary insured_____

Policy number_____

Health benefit plan_____Customer service _____

I, _____, the parent having legal cus-

tody or legal guardian of the above named child authorize any of the following adults,

_____

_____

_____

to consent to any X-ray examination, anesthetic, medical or surgical diagnosis or treatment, and hospital care, to be rendered to the minor under the general or special supervision and on the advice of any physician or surgeon licensed to practice, and to consent to any X-ray examination, anesthetic, dental or surgical diagnosis or treatment, and hospital care, to be rendered to the minor by any dentist licensed to practice.

_____

Signature of parent or legal guardian   Date

Notarized by:

State of:

Commission expires:

*Check with your physician for any special requirements for your state.

Host a Summer Survival Seminar in Your Area

In this fun, interactive seminar, attendees learn tried-and-true strategies for planning a super summer, helping kids grow in positive ways, exploring and learning new things together, and making positive memories that will last a lifetime. Meet other moms in your area and together learn:

- great crafts and activities to keep kids creatively breaking the bank
- how to turn tedium into joy with activities that teach skills and values
- ways to make family travel a rewarding adventure instead of a harrowing ordeal
- how to plan and coordinate your family's best summer ever!

This summer can be a record breaker—one in which you hear a record low of those seven dreaded words: "Mom, I'm bored. What can I do?"

Visit www.familymanager.com to learn more about scheduling Kathy Peel for a Summer Survival Seminar.

You can also request a *Presenter's Guide* if you are interested in leading a seminar for moms in your area.

About the Author

Kathy Peel has been described as "America's Family Manager" by journalists and millions of readers. She is founder and president of Family Manager, Inc., a company committed to providing helpful resources to strengthen busy families and enhance the home. She has written 18 books, which have sold over 2 million copies, including *The Family Manager Saves the Day, The Family Manager Takes Charge, Family for Life, Be Your Best, The Family Manager's Everyday Survival Guide,* and *Discover Your Destiny.*

Kathy is a popular speaker at conferences, corporate events, and churches. She has served as contributing editor to Family Circle magazine for over 12 years and also writes for other magazines. She is frequently interviewed as an expert on women's health and stress issues, home and family management, life balance and time management, and parenting. Kathy has appeared on hundreds of television and radio programs, including Oprah, Good Morning America, Today, The Early Show, CNN, MSNBC, HGTV, The Discovery Channel, The Fine Living Network, and Focus on the Family, and has been featured in hundreds of newspapers and magazines, including *Reader's Digest, Ladies Home Journal, Redbook, Women's Day, Parenting, Parents, Working Mother, InStyle, Child, Entrepreneur, Business Week,* and *Today's Christian Woman.* She is listed in Who's Who in Media.

She serves as America Online's Family and Kids Coach and been the spokesperson for many quality products and services of interest to women and families.

Kathy has been married for 34 years and is the mother of three grown sons. She lives in Dallas.

notes